Democratic Transitions

Democratic transitions have occurred in many countries in various regions across the globe, such as Southern Europe, Latin America, Africa, East and Southeast Asia, Eastern Europe and the Middle East, and these nations have undergone simultaneously political, economic and social transformations. Yet, the patterns and characteristics of transitions have varied significantly, and different modes of transition have resulted in different outcomes.

This book offers cross-national comparisons of democratic transition since the turn of the twentieth century and asks what makes democracies succeed or fail. In doing so it explores the influence the mode of transition has on the longevity or durability of the democracy, by theoretically examining and quantitatively testing this relationship. The authors argue that the mode of transition directly impacts the success and failure of democracy, and suggest that cooperative transitions, where opposition groups work together with incumbent elites to peacefully transition the state, result in democracies that last longer and are associated with higher measures of democratic quality.

Based on a cross-national dataset of all democratic transitioning states since 1900, this book will be of great interest to students and scholars of international politics, comparative politics and democracy, and democratization studies.

Sujian Guo is Distinguished Professor at Zhejiang University and Fudan University, and an academic committee member of Peking University-Fudan University-Jilin University Co-innovation Center for State Governance in China and Professor in the Department of Political Science and Director of the Center for U.S.–China Policy Studies at San Francisco State University, U.S.A.

Gary A. Stradiotto is Professorial Lecturer of Political Science at The George Washington University, U.S.A.

Democratization Studies
(formerly Democratization Studies, Frank Cass)

Democratization Studies combines theoretical and comparative studies with detailed analyses of issues central to democratic progress and its performance, all over the world.

The books in this series aim to encourage debate on the many aspects of democratization that are of interest to policy-makers, administrators and journalists, aid and development personnel, as well as to all those involved in education.

1 **Democratization and the Media**
   Edited by Vicky Randall

2 **The Resilience of Democracy**
   Persistent practice, durable idea
   Edited by Peter Burnell and Peter Calvert

3 **The Internet, Democracy and Democratization**
   Edited by Peter Ferdinand

4 **Party Development and Democratic Change in Post-Communist Europe**
   Edited by Paul Lewis

5 **Democracy Assistance**
   International co-operation for democratization
   Edited by Peter Burnell

6 **Opposition and Democracy in South Africa**
   Edited by Roger Southall

7 **The European Union and Democracy Promotion**
   The case of North Africa
   Edited by Richard Gillespie and Richard Youngs

8 **Democratization and the Judiciary**
   Edited by Siri Gloppen, Roberto Gargarella and Elin Skaar

9 **Civil Society in Democratization**
Edited by Peter Burnell and Peter Calvert

10 **The Internet and Politics**
Citizens, voters and activists
Edited by Sarah Oates, Diana Owen and Rachel Gibson

11 **Democratization in the Muslim World**
Changing patterns of authority and power
Edited by Frederic Volpi and Francesco Cavatorta

12 **Global Democracy: For and Against**
Ethical theory, institutional design and social struggles
Raffaele Marchetti

13 **Constructing Democracy in Southern Europe**
A comparative analysis of Italy, Spain and Turkey
Lauren M. McLaren

14 **The Consolidation of Democracy**
Comparing Europe and Latin America
Carsten Q. Schneider

15 **New Challenges to Democratization**
Edited by Peter Burnell and Richard Youngs

16 **Multiple Democracies in Europe**
Political culture in new member states
Paul Blokker

17 **Globality, Democracy and Civil Society**
Edited by Terrell Carver and Jens Bartelson

18 **Democracy Promotion and Conflict-based Reconstruction**
The United States and democratic consolidation in Bosnia and Afghanistan
Matthew Alan Hill

19 **Requisites of Democracy**
Conceptualization, measurement, and explanation
Jørgen Møller and Svend-Erik Skaaning

20 **The Conceptual Politics of Democracy Promotion**
Edited by Christopher Hobson and Milja Kurki

21 **Ethnic Politics and Democratic Transition in Rwanda**
David Kiwuwa

22 Democracy and Democratization in Comparative Perspective
Conceptions, conjunctures, causes and consequences
Jørgen Møller and Svend-Erik Skaaning

23 The Comparative International Politics of Democracy Promotion
Jonas Wolff, Hans-Joachim Spanger and Hans-Jürgen Puhle

24 Democratization and Ethnic Minorities
Conflict or compromise?
Edited by Jacques Bertrand and Oded Haklai

25 Democratic Transitions
Modes and outcomes
Sujian Guo and Gary A. Stradiotto

Democratic Transitions

Modes and outcomes

Sujian Guo and Gary A. Stradiotto

LONDON AND NEW YORK

First published 2014
by Routledge
2 Park Square, Milton Park, Abingdon, Oxon OX14 4RN

and by Routledge
711 Third Avenue, New York, NY 10017

Routledge is an imprint of the Taylor & Francis Group, an informa business

First issued in paperback 2016

British Library Cataloguing in Publication Data
A catalogue record for this book is available from the British Library.

Library of Congress Cataloging in Publication Data
Stradiotto, Gary A.
Democratic transitions: modes and outcomes/Gary A. Stradiotto, Sujian Guo.
  pages cm. – (Democratization studies)
  Includes bibliographical references and index.
  1. Democratization–Cross-cultural studies. I. Guo, Sujian. II. Title.
  JC423.S863 2014
  321.8–dc23

2013037826

ISBN13: 978-0-415-64320-7 (hbk)
ISBN13: 978-1-138-68355-6 (pbk)

Typeset in Times New Roman
by Wearset Ltd, Boldon, Tyne and Wear

Contents

List of figures		viii
List of tables		ix
About the authors		x
1	Introduction	1
2	Modes of democratic transition	16
3	A theory of explaining the success rate of democratic transitions	32
4	Research design and empirics	51
5	Democratic prospects	78
6	Conclusion	119
	Appendix	125
	Index	134

Figures

1.1   Average democratic duration by transition type   8
1.2   Average democratic quality by transition type   8
2.1   The process of democratization   16
3.1   Classifying transitions   33
3.2   Modes of transition, a unified approach   44
3.3   Mode of transition as intervening variable   46
3.4   Prototype democratic growth after transition   47
4.1   Research design   63
4.2   Kaplan–Meier survival estimates, by transition type   65

Tables

1.1	Summary statistics of transition type	7
4.1	Dependent and independent variable coding rules	58
4.2	OLS regression for democratic quality – ten years after transition (robust standard errors in parentheses)	66
4.3	Duration analysis for democratic longevity – ten years after transition	67
4.4	Multinomial logistic regression results of prior regime type on transition type (robust standard errors)	71
4.5	OLS results for democratic quality – prior regime type (robust standard errors)	73
4.6	Duration analysis results – prior regime type (robust standard errors)	74
5.1	The predicted value model of Iraq's democratic transition	83
5.2	The predicted value model of Tunisia's democratic transition	99
5.3	The predicted value model of Egypt's democratic transition	102
5.4	The predicted value model of Libya's democratic transition	104
5.5	The predicted value model of Yemen's democratic transition	106
5.6	China's share of world GDP	109
5.7	The predicted value model of China's potential democratic transition	113

About the authors

Professor Sujian Guo is tenured full Professor in the Department of Political Science and Director of the Center for U.S.–China Policy Studies at San Francisco State University (U.S.A.), editor-in-chief of the *Journal of Chinese Political Science* (U.S.A.), editor of Rowman & Littlefield-Lexington (U.S.A.)'s book series "Challenges Facing Chinese Political Development," director of the SFSU-Peking University Summer Programs, advisory board member of Palgrave Macmillan's book series on *China in Transformation*, and former president of the Association of Chinese Political Studies (U.S.A.). Concurrently, Dr. Guo is Distinguished Professor of Zhejiang University, Distinguished Professor of Fudan University, Associate Dean of Fudan Institute for Advanced Study in Social Sciences, Editor-in-Chief of the *Fudan Journal of the Humanities and Social Sciences*, member of editorial boards of *China Social Sciences Quarterly* and *Rediscovering China series.* Dr. Guo is also guest professor of many other academic institutions in China, such as the Center for Chinese Foreign Policy at Fudan University, Center for Public Policy at Zhejiang University, Renmin University of China, North China University, Inner Mongolia University, and Guizhou University in China. His areas of specialization include comparative politics, international relations and methodology. His research interests have focused on China/Asian politics, U.S.–China relations, international relations of East Asia, communist and post-communist studies, democratic transition, and political economy of East and Southeast Asia. He has published more than 40 academic articles both in English and Chinese (over ten articles published in SSCI journals). His authored and edited 17 books include *Chinese Politics and Government: Power, Ideology and Organization* (2012), *The State of Field: Political Science and Chinese Political Studies* (2012), *Civil Society and Governance in China* (2012), *China's Search for Good Governance* (2011), *Reviving Legitimacy: Lessons for and from China* (2011), *China's Environmental Crisis: Domestic and Global Political Responses and Impacts* (2010), *Thirty Years of China–US Relations: Analytical Approaches and Contemporary Issues* (2010), *Environmental Protection Policy and Experience in the U.S. and China's Western Regions* (2010), *Greater China in an Era of Globalization* (2009); *China in Search of a Harmonious Society* (2008); *Harmonious*

World and China's New Foreign Policy (2008), *Challenges Facing Chinese Political Development* (2007), *New Dimensions of Chinese Foreign Policy* (2007), *China in the Twenty-First Century: Challenges and Opportunities* (2007), *The Political Economy of Asian Transition from Communism* (2006), *China's "Peaceful Rise" in the 21st Century: Domestic and International Conditions* (2006); and *Post-Mao China: From Totalitarianism to Authoritarianism?* (2000). His book on *Chinese Politics and Government* was published by Routledge in 2012.

Dr. Gary A. Stradiotto is Professorial Lecturer of Political Science at the George Washington University in Washington DC, U.S.A. He is also a director at the American Red Cross. His research interests focus on democratization regime transitions, political economy, and post-communist studies. His various publications include authored and co-authored articles on democratic transition in Iraq and third wave countries, and market socialism and reform in North Korea.

1 Introduction

What determines the success or failure of nation-states transitioning to democracy? Since the American Revolution and establishment of representative government in the United States in the late eighteenth century, hundreds of countries have made the transition to democracy, most notably over the past 100 years. Democratic transitions have occurred in many countries in various regions across the globe, such as Southern Europe, Latin America, Africa, East and Southeast Asia, Eastern Europe and the Middle East. These nations have undergone simultaneously political, economic and social transformations. *Yet, the patterns and characteristics of transitions have varied significantly, and different modes of transition have resulted in different outcomes.* In some nations, democracy is implemented with minimal effort, while in others it comes at a high price and is short-lived. While some transitions have succeeded, many have failed, and collapsed dictatorships are often replaced with new dictators who are more brutal and repressive than their predecessors. Yet, other countries seem to vacillate in their democratic experiment, stuck in transitions that are never fully completed, sometimes expanding political freedoms and then contracting them (Rudra 2005, 704). To understand these divergent outcomes, in this book we seek to examine the ways that states transition to democracy and the impact this has on the success of democracy. That is, do the characteristics and patterns of democratic transitions help us predict which countries will succeed and which are at risk of failure?

The general consensus in the literature suggests that the mode of transition explains the shape the new democracy will take upon emersion and whether or not it is likely to consolidate. A democratic transition – the process of progressing the state from dictatorship to representative government – is a defining moment for a new democracy, and the mode of transition helps to shape the new democracy and affect its ability to consolidate (Munck and Leff 1997). Although scholars offer competing claims, most agree that the patterns and characteristics of the transitional process (i.e., the modes of transition) have a major impact on the prospect for democratic consolidation, because the mode of transition produces different arrangements and different types of democratic regimes. For example, electoral laws or systems, once adopted, encourage some political interests to enter into politics while at the same time discouraging others. The transitional period is often associated with crafting economic models and institutional arrangements both of which could become patterns and norms that are difficult to change later. Further, political arrangements shaped by the transition can either promote competition and the rule of law or be deficient in important areas. Whereas successful transitions encourage political stability, the rule of law and protected property rights, transitions marred by the suppression of competition will lead to political instability and likely a reversion to authoritarianism.[1]

The regime transition

A regime transition is the "interval between one political regime and another" (O'Donnell and Schmitter 1986, 6). This could mean the interval between an authoritarian polity and a democratic one, or an authoritarian polity and another authoritarian polity. A democratic transition is therefore the interval between an authoritarian polity and a democratic one. In defining the process of democratic transition, the *transfer of power* is a key element, in addition to political authority being derived from the free decision of an electorate (Linz 1990; Przeworski 1986; Welsh 1994). *Transition* refers to the intermediate phase that begins with the dissolution of an old regime and ends with the establishment of a new one (Cortona 1991). Democratic transitions consist of two simultaneous but to some extent autonomous processes: a process of dissolution of the authoritarian regime and a process of emergence of democratic institutions (Przeworski 1986; Welsh 1994).

> The key difference between authoritarian regimes and their democratic successors is that the rules of the latter guarantee opposition groups the right to challenge incumbent leaders and policies, and to replace those leaders through competitive elections. Such competition assumes broad suffrage rights, free speech and association, and guarantees of basic civil liberties. Democratic transitions can be considered to have occurred when authoritarian governments are forced to yield power to ones that operate within this set of rules.
>
> (Haggard and Kaufman, 1995)

The focus on transitions

States transition to democracy in distinct ways. Some transitions are violent (such as the popular uprising in Romania to overthrow the Ceaușescu regime in 1989, or the removal of the election-stealing dictator Noriega in Panama in 1990, which we refer to as regime collapse and foreign intervention respectively), while others are peaceful (such as the incumbent-led transition by the ruling elite in Taiwan, or the cooperative transition (or "pacted transition") in South Korea in the mid-1980s). While the goal of all democratic transitions is presumably the same – a consolidated democracy, some states arrive there more easily than others. Whitehead (2002, 45) notes:

Some democratic leaders believe they have such a clear understanding of the endpoint they have agreed to reach that they would like to proceed directly from the demise of the authoritarian regime to the unveiling of a consolidated democracy without undergoing the dramatic tensions and distracting uncertainties of the intervening transition period.

Democratic transitions are rarely easy and do not occur quickly. The transitional path has consequences for the success of democracy in the post-transitional environment. Revolutions, for example, as in Iran in 1979, the Philippines in 1986 and Romania in 1989 were abrupt and characterized by a snowballing effect. Once a political opening occurs, often through mass protests and/or armed forces defection that gain momentum, the goal of the revolution becomes clear – to remove the *ancien régime*. The unsettled business is what should replace the dictatorship. All interested parties in Iran, the Philippines and Romania agreed that the incumbent rulers had to be removed and protestors united to oust them. However, there was no consensus on what should replace them: democracy, theocracy, or a new dictator. In Romania, where there was no preceding process of liberalization and where a quick outburst of popular uprising toppled the old regime, a provisional government was formed "whose plans [were] uncertain and might not lead to a democracy" (Linz 1990, 156). In these cases, the revolution was the first step in the transition, but the continued transitional process was necessary to settle the unfinished business of the abrupt collapse. Many of these states (e.g., the Philippines and Romania) continue to this day to inch towards a consolidated democratic system.

Alternatively, peaceful and negotiated transitions are characterized by a duality of purpose – to remove or reform the existing regime and replace it with something more democratic. The purpose and outcome of roundtable discussions (such as Hungary in 1989–90) were to transition the state to democracy, which all parties in the negotiations agreed upon. Both violent and peaceful transitions concur that the incumbent regime must be removed or reformed, yet only in peaceful transitions is it clear that the replacement should be democratic – the evidence supports this as we discuss in Chapter 3. Knowing where you are going facilitates democratic success; a troublesome issue with revolution is that while opposition groups unite to overthrow incumbent regimes, they often fracture after removal and then bargain for their desired outcome in the new regime. Often that is democracy and free elections; however, instances exist where certain opposition groups instrumental in regime overthrow contain a distinct power advantage during the transitional process and use it to subvert democracy and install the government of their choice (e.g., Iran in 1979 where pro democracy reformers lost out to hard line theologians).

In peaceful transitions, power advantage is important. Where powerful incumbents negotiate a democratic opening, they may attempt to use their leverage to design electoral rules that benefit them the most under a democratic system. We refer to these transitions as "conversion." As the name implies, the incumbents attempt to convert the existing regime into a democratic polity, albeit one that favors their continued rule. On the other hand, where opposition groups unite in their quest for democracy while incumbents are willing to work with opposition groups, the evidence suggests that democracy is most likely to flourish as the institutions adopted are more inclusive and therefore conducive to competition, a core tenet of representative government. We refer to these transitions as "cooperative." Thus, the transition to democracy and the path taken have profound implications on whether or not democracy succeeds or fails. The empirical evidence presented in Chapter 4 will overwhelmingly show that cooperative transitions are the most conducive to democratic success.

Yet, despite the implications for successful and sustainable democracy, little is empirically known about how transition type affects democracy, i.e., few studies have quantitatively tested the empirical relationship between modes of transition and democratic outcomes. As a defining event, the legacy of the transition lasts long after the process of democratization ends. In telling the story of democracy, we link the process of transition to the likelihood of democratic survival. Successful transitions result in successful democracies whereas problematic transitions result in democracies that either muddle along and stagnate or revert to autocracy. Understanding the dynamics and mechanisms of the transition process places us in a better position to understand why democracy succeeds and/or fails.

The debate on transitions

According to Przeworski (1991), "The strategic problem of transition is to get to democracy without being either killed by those who have arms or starved by those who control productive resources ... the final destination depends on the path" (51). The path is the nature and characteristics of the transition that leads to democratic success or failure. According to scholars who advocate a path dependency analysis of democratization, the mode of transition from authoritarian rule has implications for the prospects of democratic consolidation (Linz 1981; O'Donnell and Schmitter 1986; Karl 1990; Di Palma 1990; Huntington 1991; Karl and Schmitter 1991; Przeworski 1991; O'Donnell 1992; Linz and Stepan 1996; Munck and Leff 1997). Due to its effects on the post-transitional regime and on the pattern of elite competition, the institutional rules crafted during the transition and elites' acceptance or rejection of these rules are formative (Munck and Leff 1997, 345). Institutions are instrumental not only because they create efficiency in governance, but also because they have profound distributional effects (Knight 1992). Yet, concerning the importance of the transitional process, consensus ends here.

The debate among scholars of democratization centers on the perceived merits of certain transitional modes over others. For example, the democratization literature reveals some general hypotheses about the effects of *pacted* transitions (Field 2005, 1080). According to O'Donnell and Schmitter (1986) a *pact* is an "explicit, but not always explicated or justified, agreement among a select set of actors which seeks to define (or, better, to redefine) rules governing the exercise of power on the basis of mutual guarantees for the 'vital interests' of those entering into it" (37). For purposes of our argument, we define a pact more generally as:

> A process involving a negotiating unit comprised of incumbent and opposition groups attempting to peacefully bargain the transition away from authoritarian rule to democracy.

Incumbents refer to those in positions of power while opposition groups refer to those opposed to the status quo. The number and strength of incumbents and opposition groups varies tremendously between transitions. While we agree that pacts are essentially explicit agreements among elite actors attempting to transition the state, we view these as peaceful attempts at the transitional process, compared to the more violent method of revolution. Some scholars argue that pacted transitions are more likely to result in consolidated democracies than other transition types (O'Donnell and Schmitter 1986; Karl 1990; Karl and Schmitter 1991). According to O'Donnell and Schmitter (1986) "Pacts ... are desirable [and] enhance the probability that the process will lead to a viable political democracy" (39). Similarly, pacts "are meant to accommodate 'vital interests' and, therefore, facilitate the installation of democracy" (1080). O'Donnell and Schmitter point out that, "with the exception of Costa Rica, all of the unpacted democracies existing at different times in other Latin American countries were destroyed by authoritarian reversals" (45). Karl and Schmitter (1991) insist that the most successful formula for democratic transition has been the negotiation of pacts among elites. Similarly, Huntington (1991) suggests that pacts have been valuable tools in managing democratic transitions (276).

Others contend that pacted transitions are characterized by the suppression of competition and therefore impede the consolidation and progression of democracy (Karl 1987; Przeworski 1991; Hagopian 1996).[2] Field (2004) notes that "Much of the literature on pact-making and pacted transitions claims [they] depress access to positions of political leadership" (1). Przeworski (1991), in discussing the danger of pacts, argues

> ...they will become cartels of incumbents against contenders, cartels that restrict competition, bar access, and distribute the benefits of political power among the insiders. Democracy would then turn into a private project of leaders of some political parties and corporatist associations, an oligopoly in which leaders of some organizations collude to prevent outsiders from entering.
>
> (90–91)

When the relation of transitional forces is uncertain, Przeworski (1991) argues "...institutions are custom-made for a particular person, party, or alliance" (82). This would seem to lead to exclusionary mechanisms in the political process; not a desirable outcome for a new democracy. Karl (1987) further suggests that pacts tend to demobilize new social forces and circumscribe the participation of certain actors, thereby producing a "frozen democracy" (88). Field (2005) speculates that pacts may result in "the reduction of competitiveness [and] may also have a direct impact on policy making" (1080).

Hagopian (1990) demonstrates that a fragile democracy such as Brazil, with a weak democratic tradition and two decades of military rule, cannot be consolidated and extended by political pacts alone (153). She argues that political pacts bargained by elites that made the regime transition possible actually limited the extension of democracy. By restoring many sources of their political power to old regime elites in exchange for their support of democratization, political pacts left the military with a substantial power over civilians. This preservation of clientelism undermined the ability of political parties to transform themselves into genuine transmission belts for non-elite interests (147). Hagopian (1990) concludes that "in Brazil pacts did not broaden and deepen democracy, nor did the politicians who forged them create strong democratic institutions and resolve to adhere to democratic political practices" (166). Thus, democracy initiated by political pact does not always result in democratic consolidation. In many instances, it produces the opposite effect.

Still others argue transition through revolution or breakdown of the *ancien régime* is the least problematic transition type due to the opposition being able to impose demands for unrestricted elections and the inability of the old elites to interfere in the democratization process. Karl and Schmitter (1991) argue that revolutions produce enduring patterns of domination but not necessarily democratic ones, while according to Munck and Leff (1997), *reform through rupture* (i.e., revolution) is the least difficult type of transition since it results in a complete break from the past and allows the opposition unrestricted elections. The rapidity of the transformation to democracy, however, may reduce incentives for elites to foster cooperative relationships and consensus.

An important contribution of this study is empirically testing these conflicting accounts. We progress the literature to its next logical step – cross-national statistical analyses that incorporate the various approaches. This allows us to assess the merits of the aforementioned claims.[3] This book will proceed under the following assumptions: (1) regime transitions occur through a variety of ways that can be specified and categorized into four types; (2) consensus exists that the mode of transition directly affects the prospects of democratic consolidation – that some modes are more likely to lead to democratic deepening than others; (3) that it is possible to conceptualize and measure democratic quality and duration and empirically test it against any given mode of transition, and (4) identifying problematic transitions helps us to understand the dynamics most likely to lead to democratic breakdown and the reversion to authoritarianism. In this study, we explore (1) and (3). Assumption (2) is taken for granted and (4) is an area left for future research.

Our study is situated within the transitions literature and builds upon the important works of earlier scholars. We show that transitions not only matter but that they are highly relevant and constitute "formative and defining moments."

However, in order to determine whether transitions "matter," two complimentary questions are necessary:

1 *Is post-transition democratic survival or duration a function of the mode of transition? That is, are some modes of transition more likely than others to result in democratic survival or a reversion to authoritarian rule?*
2 *Does the way in which states transition to democracy impact democratic quality? That is, do certain types of transition result in a more rapid democratic deepening than others?*

By "matter", we employ two key indicators to capture intent: *quality and duration.* For transitions to matter, they must affect both the *quality* and the *survivability* of democracy. The bifurcation of these issues is important since duration is not synonymous with quality and some democracies achieve a rapid deepening despite being democratic for only a few years.

Summary statistics are a useful starting point to understand the importance of transition type on democracy. Table 1.1 depicts summary statistics for the four transition types. Most notable is that out of 128 nations, 37 since 1900 transitioned by cooperative pacts and only two (5 percent) reverted to dictatorship.[4] This is in stark contrast to transition by conversion where out of 48 cases, 22 (46 percent) failed. Further, cooperative transitions have an average ten-year polity score of 7.76. While foreign interventions result in higher average polity scores, only one-third of the cases are cooperative transitions. We suspect that foreign interventions are driven by the remarkable results of post-World War II liberations and are therefore inflated. Transition by conversion has an average Polity IV score of only 4.60.[5]

In Figure 1.1, it can be seen that cooperative transitions are also associated with a longer democratic duration, almost ten years (we measure survivability for ten years after the transition, so Figure 1.1 shows that cooperative transitions survive almost the entire time). Ten years is not an arbitrary cut-off point. In the dataset, only one country (Greece 1926) survived as a democracy for ten years and then reverted to dictatorship. Thus, once a state has remained democratic for ten years, the possibility of reversion is significantly diminished. This finding is consistent with a study by Svolik (2008) who quantitatively demonstrates that the age of a democracy is associated with an increase in the odds of its survival

Table 1.1 Summary statistics of transition type

Transition type	N	Reversions	Percent reversions	10-year Polity rating
Conversion	48	22	46	4.60
Cooperative	37	2	5	7.76
Collapse	31	10	32	5.84
Foreign intervention	12	3	25	8.25
Totals	128	37	29	

(155). The implication is logical – the longer a democracy survives; the chance of reversion grows smaller with each passing year. This is in stark contrast to empirical literature on transitions that finds no statistical evidence that the age of a democracy is associated with greater chances of its survival (see, e.g., Epstein *et al.* 2006; Przeworski *et al.* 2000). A large part of the disparity in the findings of the various studies, including this one, is a direct result of measuring democracy by varying standards and indices. Until a consistent measurement criterion is established, the conjectures are likely to vary by the number of studies.

Figure 1.2 provides additional supporting evidence to the summary statistics. Cooperative transitions are associated with higher democratic quality ratings than other transition types except foreign intervention (there have only been 12

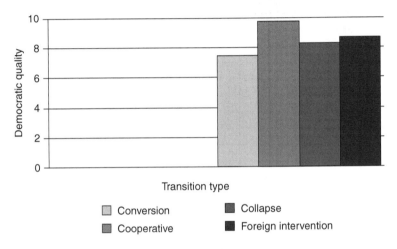

Figure 1.1 Average democratic duration by transition type.

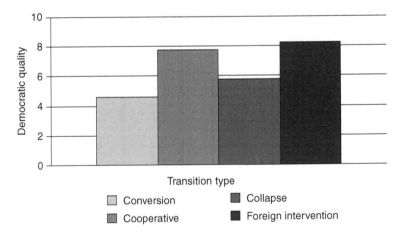

Figure 1.2 Average democratic quality by transition type.

foreign intervention cases since 1900 and most are associated with World War II liberations). In reviewing the summary statistics, one discernable pattern emerges: cooperative transitions are quite favorable to democratic success. Not only do cooperative transitions result in higher average levels of democracy and have the lowest reversion rate, they also last longer. In the theoretical chapter, we flesh this out.

Importance

Understanding transitions remains an important area of scholarly inquiry. First, a large part of the world is undemocratic, and many countries are gripped by authoritarian regimes, often brutal and repressive. Next, the transition literature falls short in creating generalizable conclusions about the influence of transitional mode on democracy. We attempt to understand systematic and explicable patterns of transitional legacies and create generalizable conclusions regarding modes of transition on the success of democracy. This project constitutes a first step in identifying problematic transitions in order to understand the unique circumstances that accompany democratic breakdown and also builds upon the important works of earlier scholars.

The literature consists mostly of case studies and is regionally focused. Although case studies provide the nuances that larger-n statistical analyses cannot, "the single observation is not a useful technique for testing hypotheses or theories" (King, Keohane and Verba 1996, 211), and to date, no large-n cross-national statistical analyses of democratic transitional modes exist. Therefore, advancing the state of the literature on democratization to robust statistical cross-national analyses provides a new and important contribution to the literature.

The literature on democratic transitions was abundant in the 1980s and early 1990s but once Latin America and Eastern Europe made the transition to democracy, scholars turned their attention to issues of consolidation (e.g., Encarnación 2000; Mainwaring and Scully 1995; Jelin and Hershberg 1996; Morlino 1998). In doing so, the agenda on democratic transitions was pushed aside.[6] The opportunity for generalizable conclusions was shelved, and while many states reverted to authoritarian rule, the focus remained on the states that succeeded. According to Higley and Burton (1989), the volume of work on democratization "offers no sound theoretical basis for judging the survival prospects of newly democratic regimes" (17). In this study, we seek to do just that.

Returning to the process of transition enables us to build on the foundation laid by earlier scholars, and to move away from a country and regional focus. Only then can our findings be applied to future transitioning states with greater certainty. We will also see the link between transition and consolidation; one cannot be discussed without the other, and transitions directly affect the prospects for democratic survivability.

This study makes three significant contributions to the literature. First, transitions are both "defining and formative" events that have lasting consequences on the quality and duration of democracy. We attempt to progress the literature towards solving an important debate among scholars as to whether modes of transition matter by developing a comparative and statistical methodology to empirically test hypotheses. Second, we create a conceptual categorization from which to classify transitioning states (i.e., an in depth discussion on modes of transition). Third, we develop a rigorous theoretical explanation as to why certain modes of transition are the most viable path to democratic consolidation.

Through an analysis of transition type and the equality of competition that emerges from negotiations between incumbents and elites, we describe systematic patterns of transitional legacies and derive generalizable conclusions from the modes of transition on the success of democracy. This project constitutes a first step in identifying problematic transitions in order to understand the circumstances that accompany democratic breakdown. Examining democratic transitions cross-nationally and temporally allows us to create generalizations about the transitional process and to distinguish a successful from an unsuccessful transition.

A project on democratic transitions is interesting on numerous grounds. Political democracy permits the greatest level of individual freedom and normatively this is a worthwhile objective. Increased civil liberties, freedom from arbitrary persecution, expanded political freedoms and the pursuit of liberty are more desirable compared to non-democratic regimes, characterized by arbitrary and unfair laws. Democracies also tend to be less violent than dictatorships in their relations with other democracies, a core proposition of democratic peace arguments. From an international politics perspective, securing democracy around the world is a means of reducing global conflict and increasing cooperation. Democratic peace theorists note a powerful empirical generalization: democracies rarely go to war with one another (Babst 1972; Levy 1988; Maoz and Abdolali 1989; Maoz and Russett 1993; Russett 1993). The more democratic a dyad of states is, the less likely they are to be involved in conflict (Bueno de Mesquita and Lalman 1992; Kegley and Hermann 1995).

This project builds on our understanding of democratic transitions in numerous ways. First, this study attempts to move us towards settling an important debate as to whether modes of transition matter. Prior scholarship raised the question and opened the debate on the merits and relevance of transitional modes. We show that transitions are highly relevant and have lasting consequences on the quality and duration of a democracy. Second, we create a parsimonious typology by which to classify transitioning states. This classification scheme allows for a new and consistent methodology in the categorization of transitioning states. Third, we develop a rigorous theoretical explanation as to why cooperative transitions are the most viable path to democratic installation. Implicit in our argument is the importance of examining institutional choice in the new democracy along with the actors who make the choices during the transition. Fourth, we create a dataset that classifies all democratic transitions since 1900, along with corresponding democratic quality ratings and annual economic growth rates. By advancing our understanding of transitions, it will be easier to determine the reasons democracy succeeds, or why it fails.

Chapter outlines

Chapter 1 discusses the puzzle in our study on democratic transitions, focusing on the questions: (1) Is democratic survival or duration in post-transition a function of the mode of transition? That is, are some modes of transition more likely than others to result in democratic survival or reversion to authoritarian rule? and (2) Does the way in which states transition to democracy impact democratic duration and quality? That is, do certain types of transition result in a more rapid democratic deepening than others?

Our study is situated within the transitions literature and builds upon the important works of earlier scholars who examined the effects of transitional types on democratic outcomes. We also discuss our theoretical assumptions that are derived from the transition literature and our empirical observations. This leads us to formulate empirical hypotheses that can be tested against our dataset on transitioning states. The significance of answering these questions in democratic transition scholarship, and the necessity of empirically testing the hypotheses derived from our theory helps us to explain the success rate of democratic transitions across a large number of cases.

Chapter 2 introduces and reviews the literature on democratic transitions and modes of transition. We define transitions and categorize transitioning states along a continuum ranging from peaceful to violent.

Chapter 3 is concerned with theory development that would explain the success rate of democratic transitions, in addition to developing hypotheses for testing. We argue that cooperative transitions offer the greatest promise of democratic success. The reasons for this are the emergence of an inclusive and balanced pattern of elite competition in the new democracy. Where inclusive competition is encouraged and respected, democracy is more likely to succeed. Where inclusive competition is suppressed and opposition groups have a difficult time finding a place in the new government, democracy tends to stagnate and eventually revert. When incumbents and opposition groups work together to create a peaceful transition, it is more likely for the regime to tolerate the opposition, and advance mutual interests on the playing field of democratic transition. Transitions marked by violence have a difficult time moving forward. The use of force during the transitional period spills over into the new democracy as a practical way of solving problems (Ward and Gleditsch 1998). Chairman of Freedom House, Peter Ackerman (2007) suggests "there [is] more than a three-to-one chance that a country in transition would attain a high freedom rating post-transition if the opposition to dictatorship did not employ violent force" (4).

In Chapter 4, we discuss the research design and dataset, including decision rules on coding cases and sources for obtaining democratic quality and longevity ratings, and quantitatively testing the hypotheses deduced from our theory in explaining the success rate of democratic transitions. We rely on qualitative historical analysis of the events in the countries under study, in addition to accepted datasets on transitioning states. We then test our arguments through statistical analyses. First, we test the hypothesis that cooperative transitions, in which opposition groups and incumbents work together, are associated with higher levels of democracy and last longer than other transition types. The results strongly confirm this hypothesis. Next, we test Geddes' (1999) contention that prior regime type determines transition type, which poses a challenge to the independent effects of transition type on democracy. We find that under an expanded dataset, the results break down. That is, prior regime type does not dictate the transition path available to states. The cumulative effects of these findings, including various robustness checks, allow us to conclude that transition type is a defining and formative event and that the way states transition from dictatorship has a strong effect on the quality and longevity of democracy.

In Chapter 5, we examine the prospects for successful democracy through predicted value probability analysis in various countries that have recently initiated a process of transition and also provide some case studies on the mode of transition in Iraq, Tunisia, Egypt, Libya and Yemen, and a case study on China, a country with the possibility of transitioning in the future.

In Chapter 6, we summarize the findings and discuss the lessons learned from this project. We highlight the contributions this study makes to the literature on transitions and outline potential areas for further research.

Notes

1 Juan J. Linz and Alfred Stepan, *Problems of Democratic Transition and Consolidation: Southern Europe, South America, and Post-Communist Europe* (Baltimore, MD, and London: The Johns Hopkins University Press, 1996); Terry L. Karl and Philippe C. Schmitter, "Modes of Transition in Latin America, Southern and Eastern Europe," in Geoffrey Pridham, ed., *Transitions to Democracy: Comparative Perspectives from Southern Europe, Latin America and Eastern Europe* (Aldershot, England: Dartmouth, 1995); O'Donnell, Schmitter, and Whitehead, ed., *Transitions from Authoritarian Rule: Southern Europe*; Larry Diamond *et al.*, ed., *Consolidating the Third Wave Democracies*, 1997; Russell Bova, "Political Dynamics of the Post-Communist Transition: A Comparative Perspective," in Frederic J. Fleron, Jr. and Erik P. Hoffmann, ed., *Post-Communist Studies & Political Science* (Boulder, CO: Westview, 1993); S.D. Muni, "Patterns of Democracy in South Asia," *International Social Science Journal*, vol. 43, no. 2, May 1991; Anek Laothamatas, ed., *Democratization in Southeast and East Asia* (New York: St. Martin, 1997).
2 Theorists also hypothesize that pacted transitions depress the level of inter-party competition and reduce mass participation and inclusion. For assessments of these claims, see Bonnie N. Field. 2002. *Frozen Democracy? Pacting and the Consolidation of Democracy: The Spanish and Argentine Democracies Compared.* Ph.D. dissertation, University of California, Santa Barbara. Encarnación.
3 Similarly to Keohane (2007), we argue for the importance of a medium n (40–60 cases) in uncovering causal relationships. The advantages of a medium n is that it allows the researcher to know many cases in depth, compared to an n of say 8,000 where the researcher simply engages in coding.
4 Reversion refers to a return to authoritarian rule or the failure of democracy. For example, a country may transition to democracy and then five years later the democracy fails and is replaced by an authoritarian regime.
5 We discuss Polity IV scores extensively in Chapter 4. Briefly, Polity scores are an

index that measure authority patterns of all nation-states. The scores allow us to determine if a regime can be considered a dictatorship or a democracy. The scores range from −10 (most authoritarian such as North Korea) to a +10 (most democratic such as the United States). We argue that Polity scores must achieve a 5 or higher to be considered a democratic polity, with a 5 representing a polity with minimalistic characteristics of democracy.

6 We do not imply that no scholars are working within the transitions literature; however, there is far less concentration on transitions than in previous years. For some excellent recent works on transitions see McFaul's (2002) World Politics article; Freedom House's study "How Freedom is Won" and works by Bonnie Field (2004, 2005) on Spain's democratic transition.

References

Ackerman, Peter. 2007. *How Freedom is won*. Conference on Democracy and Security sponsored through Freedom House. Czernin Palace, Czech Republic June 5–6.

Babst, D.V. 1972. *A Force for Peace*. Industrial Research: 14.

Bueno de Mesquita, Bruce, and David Lalman. 1992. *War and Reason: Domestic and International Imperatives*. New Haven: Yale University Press.

Di Palma, Giuseppe. 1990. *Democracies: An Essay on Democratic Transitions*. Berkeley: University of California Press.

Encarnación, O.G. 2000. "Beyond Transitions: The Politics of Democratic Consolidation." *Comparative Politics* 32(4): 479–498.

Epstein, David L., Robert Bates, Jack Goldstone, Ida Kristensen and Sharyn O'Halloran. 2006. "Democratic Transitions." *American Journal of Political Science* 50(3): 551–569.

Field, Bonnie N. 2004. "Modes of Transition, Internal Party Rules, and Levels of Elite Continuity: A Comparison of the Spanish and Argentine Democracies." *Center for the Study of Democracy at the University of California, Irvine.*

Field, Bonnie N. 2005. "De-thawing Democracy: The Decline of Political Party Collaboration in Spain (1977 to 2004)." *Comparative Political Studies* 38(9): 1079–1103.

Geddes, Barbara. 1999. "Authoritarian Breakdown: Empirical Test of a Game Theoretic Approach." *Paper prepared for the annual meeting of the American Political Science Association*, Atlanta, Georgia.

Haggard, Stephan and Robert R. Kaufman. 1995. *The Political Economy of Democratic Transitions*. New Jersey: Princeton University Press.

Hagopian, Frances. 1990. "Democracy by Undemocratic Means? Elites, Political Pacts, and Regime Transition in Brazil." *Comparative Political Studies* 23: 147–170.

Hagopian, Frances. 1996. *Traditional Politics and Regime Change in Brazil*. New York: Cambridge University Press.

Higley, John and Michael G. Burton. 1989. "The Elite Variable in Democratic Transitions and Breakdowns." *American Sociological Review* 54 (1): 17–32.

Huntington, Samuel P. 1991. *The Third Wave: Democratization in the Late Twentieth Century*. Norman: University of Oklahoma Press.

Jelin, Elizabeth and Eric Hershberg, eds. 1996. *Constructing Democracy: Human Rights, Citizenship and Society in Latin America*. Boulder, Colorado: Westview Press.

Karl, Terry Lynn. 1987. "Petroleum and Political Pacts." *Latin American Research Review* 22: 63–94.

Karl, Terry Lynn. 1990. "Dilemmas of Democratization in Latin America." *Comparative Politics* 23(1): 1–21.

Karl, Terry Lynn and Philippe C. Schmitter. 1991. "Modes of Transition in Latin America, Southern and Eastern Europe." *International Social Science Journal* 128: 269–284.

Kegley, Charles W. and Margaret G. Hermann. 1995. "The Political Psychology of Peace through Democratization." *Cooperation and Conflict* 30(1): 5–30.

Keohane, Robert O. 2007. Finding Standards for Descriptive and Causal Inference: Ongoing Debates, Part II. *Consortium on Qualitative Research Methods,* lecture given on January 3.

King, Gary, Robert O. Keohane and Sidney Verba. 1996. *Designing Social Inquiry.* Princeton: Princeton University Press.

Knight, Jack. 1992. *Institutions and Social Conflict.* Cambridge: Cambridge University Press.

Levy, Jack S. 1988. "Domestic Politics and War." *Journal of Interdisciplinary History* 18(6): 53–73.

Linz, Juan. 1981. "Some Comparative Thoughts on the Transition to Democracy in Portugal and Spain." In *Portugal since the Revolution: Economic and Political Perspectives,* ed. Jorge Braga de Macedo and Simon Serfaty. Boulder: Westview Press.

Linz, Juan. 1990. "Transitions to Democracy." *The Washington Quarterly* (Summer): 143–164.

Linz, Juan and Alfred Stepan. 1996. *Problems of Democratic Transition and Consolidation: Southern Europe, South America and Post-Communist Europe.* Baltimore: The Johns Hopkins University Press.

Mainwaring, Scott and Timothy R. Scully. 1995. *Building Democratic Institutions: Party Systems in Latin America.* Stanford: Stanford University Press.

Maoz, Zeev, and Nasrin Abdolali. 1989. "Regime Types and International Conflict, 1816–1976." *Journal of Conflict Resolution* 33(1): 3–35.

Maoz, Zeev, and Bruce Russett. 1993. "Normative and Structural Causes of Democratic Peace, 1946–1986." *American Political Science Review* 87(3): 624–638.

McFaul Michael. 2002. "The Fourth Wave of Democracy and Dictatorship: Noncooperative Transitions in the Postcommunist World." In *World Politics* vol. 54, no. 2: 212–244.

Moore, Barrington, Jr. 1966. *Social Origins of Dictatorship and Democracy.* Boston: Beacon Press.

Morlino, L. 1998. *Democracy between Consolidation and Crisis: Parties, Groups, and Citizens in Southern Europe.* Oxford, UK: Oxford University Press.

Munck, Gerardo L. and Carol Skalnik Leff. 1997. "Modes of Transition and Democratization: South American and Eastern Europe in Comparative Perspective." *Comparative Politics* 29: 343–362.

O'Donnell, Guillermo. 1992. "Transitions, Continuities, and Paradoxes." In *Issues in Democratic Consolidation: The New South American Democracies in Comparative Perspective,* ed. Scott Mainwaring, Guillermo O'Donnell and J. Samuel Valenzuela. Notre Dame: Notre Dame Press: 17–56.

O'Donnell, Guillermo and Philippe Schmitter. 1986. *Transitions from Authoritarian Rule: Tentative Conclusions about Uncertain Democracies.* Baltimore: The Johns Hopkins University Press.

Przeworski, Adam. 1986. "Some Problems in the Study of the Transition to Democracy." In *Transitions from Authoritarian Rule.* Comparative Perspectives, vol. 3, ed. O'Donnell G., Philippe Schmitter and Laurence Whitehead. Baltimore: Johns Hopkins University Press: 47–64.

Przeworski, Adam. 1991. *Democracy and the Market.* New York: Cambridge University Press.

Przeworski, Adam, Michael Alvarez, Jose Antonio Cheibub and Fernando Limongi. 2000. *Democracy and Development: Political Institutions and Well-Being in the World, 1950–1990.* New York: Cambridge University Press.

Rudra, Nita. 2005. "Globalization and the Strengthening of Democracy in the Developing World." *American Journal of Political Science* 49(4): 704–730.

Russett, Bruce M. 1993. *Grasping the Democratic Peace: Principles for a Post-Cold War World.* Princeton: Princeton University Press.

Svolik, Milan. 2008. "Authoritarian Reversals and Democratic Consolidation." *American Political Science Review* 102(2): 153–168.

Ward, Michael D. and Kristian S. Gleditsch. 1998. "Democratizing for Peace." *American Political Science Review* 92(1): 52–62.

Welsh, Helga A. 1994. "Political Transition Processes in Central and Eastern Europe." *Comparative Politics* 27 (July): 379–394.

Whitehead, Lawrence. 2002. *Democratization: Theory and Experience.* Oxford and New York: Oxford University Press.

2 Modes of democratic transition

This chapter introduces and reviews the literature on democratic transitions and modes of transition. We attempt to address some significant questions related to the process of democratization, define democratic transition and consolidation, and categorize transitional modes based on the synthesis of the rich literature on the modes of transition from authoritarianism to democracy. We advance our research agenda by pointing out the limitations of the existing literature on the effect of transitional models on democratic outcomes, because the literature is largely based on regional and country-specific studies which limit their generalizability. We utilize cross-national statistical analyses to further explore the empirical relationship between transition modes and democratic outcomes in a search for greater generalizability.

Transitions

A *regime* transition is "the interval between one political regime and another" (O'Donnell and Schmitter 1986, 6). A *democratic* transition is the interval between an authoritarian polity and a democratic one, in addition to the process by which it occurs. In this study, we are concerned with democratic transitions, which are an integral part of the democratization process. The process of democratization consists of three significant areas: (1) *why* (why do states become democratic; what are the necessary preconditions for democratic government); (2) *how* (how do states become democratic; the actual process of transition); and (3) *endurance* (how long do states stay democratic; the essence of consolidation). Along a time continuum, the process of democratization is represented as in Figure 2.1.

Thus, the starting point of democratization consists of the necessary preconditions that lead towards a transition. A successful transition then leads to the ideal end point of democratization – consolidation, or a democracy that lasts. To place

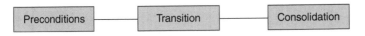

Figure 2.1 The process of democratization.

the transitional phase in its appropriate context, we briefly discuss preconditions and consolidation. This allows us to properly situate the transition within the democratization literature and explore how it is affected by preconditions and how it influences consolidation.

3 Steps of democratization

Preconditions

The first step of democratization is the diverse preconditions that cause authoritarian polities to seek democracy. The literature that examines why states become democratic is prolific, most notably rooted in the tradition of historical and comparative analysis and modernization theory. Authoritarian breakdown is often associated with regime failure, frequently due to economic collapse. The most prominent theorist who asserted that economic change leads to the rise of democracy was Karl Marx, who adopted a comparative and historical approach. To Marx (1848), the bourgeoisie (the middle or merchant class, whose status and power comes from employment, education and earned wealth), was the main agent for the rise of Western democracy. Since the old regime is authoritarian and anti-capitalistic, the bourgeoisie turns to democracy as a means of achieving political power. Max Weber agreed with Marx and posited that the poor functioning of the German parliamentary democracy during his time was attributable to the weakness of the bourgeoisie (Laothamatas 1997, 2). Barrington Moore, Jr., (1966) employed a comparative-historical analysis approach in his study, *The Social Origins of Dictatorship and Democracy*. Moore asserted "No bourgeoisie, no democracy" (418); however, his thesis suggested that lords and peasants hold the key to successful democratization. Moore's central tenet was that if landlords succeed in imposing or introducing a commercial, capitalistic order on the agricultural sector, then the ruling elite has no need for an authoritarian, repressive regime to force the rural masses into their proper place and function. Democracy is therefore possible. In contrast, if the landlords hold steadfast to the old quasi-feudalistic agrarian economy, there arises a need for a strong and repressive state. In this latter case, democracy is not acceptable to the ruling or agrarian elites.

In addition to comparative and historical analysis, the other major scholarly tradition postulating a link between economic development and democracy is modernization theory. Modernization theorists find a strong and direct relationship between economic development and democracy (Lipset 1959; Cutright 1963). In Lipset's view, democracy depends on a society's level of economic development. According to Lipset (1959), "Perhaps the most widespread generalization linking political systems to other aspects of society [is] that democracy is related to the state of economic development" (75). That is, "the more well-to-do a nation, the greater the chances that it will sustain democracy" (75). Additional studies provide empirical support for the thesis that higher levels of economic development promote democracy (Jackman 1973; Burkhart and

Lewis-Beck 1994; Londregan and Poole 1996), although the causal arrow does not seem to point in the other direction. Further, research shows the relationship is not linear; the probability of democracy does not increase automatically with the level of development. Several scholars point to the importance of a middle income range, defined in terms of per capita income (Gill 2000, 3).

Modernization theory is a structuralist approach, which focuses on macrolevel social conditions or socioeconomic and cultural prerequisites of democracy, i.e., the causal link between socioeconomic structures and political changes, and seeks to explain why countries democratize. Greater economic development leads to increased education, better communication, a more mobile way of life, greater wealth, and a growing middle class. This invariably spills over into the political arena, where competing interests vie for the state's attention and the opportunity to influence policy decisions. Social class manoeuvering is a key explanatory variable of democratization, as the populace demands democratic governance. Economic development leads to the emergence of a large number of voluntary, autonomous social organizations which not only seek to place a check on government but also to increase political participation, enhance political skills, and generate and disseminate new opinions. Rueschemeyer *et al.* (1992) argue that "capitalist development is associated with democracy because it transforms the class structure, strengthening the working and middle classes and weakening the landed upper class" (7). To them, "[t]he working class was the most consistently pro-democratic force. The class had a strong interest in effecting its political inclusion…" (8).

Scholars in the modernization tradition argue level of development also serves as a crucial factor in the viability and survivability of a democracy. The empirical evidence suggests that richer democracies rarely fail and that democracies that survive a long time are also less likely to fail (Przeworski et al., 2000, Przeworski and Limongi 1997). According to Wright (2006), "well-entrenched institutions are difficult to overturn, especially when the citizens of that country are relatively well [off]" (2). According to Przeworski (1991) "As everyone agrees, the eventual survival of the new democracies will depend to a large extent on their economic performance" (95). In a robustness test of democratic survivability, Epstein *et al.* (2006) show that "…higher GDP per capita reduces the probability that countries fall out of democracy" (564). However, correlation is not causation. The fact that democracies tend to be in affluent societies does not explain why this is the case. Alternatively, some affluent societies remain authoritarian.

There are other transition theories that seek to explain why transition occurs, and may not agree with the above theories that emphasize macro-level socioeconomic preconditions for democracy. One prominent approach is *process-driven elite strategic choice*, which emphasizes the micro-level variables, i.e., the critical role of individual elites and their strategic interaction and choice, the splits within the regime, and the power balance between "softliners" and "hardliners" in the transition process, and thus, elite choices and their strategic interactions are considered decisive in determining the outcome of transition, though they do not deny the role of socioeconomic factors (Linz and Stepan 1978; O'Donnell and Schmitter 1986; Di Palma 1990). Of central concern to this group of scholars is the process of transition rather than structural conditions. Di Palma (1990) gave special attention to the process of "democratic crafting," involving "negotiated agreements" between ruling elites and opposition elites that moved common perceptions of "self-interest" toward accepting democracy as the best possible regime form under given conditions. He argued that the game between ruling elites and opposition elites could be converted into a positive sum game, if the right steps in the process of regime transition were undertaken. Therefore, skillful crafting and tactical devices of transition were important in facilitating the transition process (Kitschelt 1996, 1032).

The process of transition

The second step of democratization is the transition itself and the focus of this research. Through what method do states become democratic, and how does this affect the quality and duration of democracy? A transition process is "...the movement from a nondemocratic to a democratic regime" (Linz and Stepan 1996, 38). Authoritarian regimes may fail in the economic sphere, lose a sense of direction, credibility, disintegrate or succumb to intense international pressure for change. Rudra (2005) suggests that a key precondition of the democratization literature resides in the disunity of political elites as a precondition for prominent political change in any nation" (705). Regardless of the impetus for change, transition paths vary greatly by country, as do the outcomes. Further, the break-down of an authoritarian regime is not always followed by the establishment of a democratic one. We discuss the process of transition below.

The method that a state uses to transform itself from an authoritarian polity into a democratic one defines the transitional process. Historical analysis tells us that the emergence of democracy is characterized by abrupt social, economic and political change. Just as democracies around the globe have different character-istics, so does the path by which states become democratic. That is, states become democratic through a variety of means. This leads us to expand the defi-nition of a democratic transition as:

> Democratic transition refers to a political process of movement aimed at establishing a democratic political system, initiated either from above (elite driven) or below (mass driven) or a combination of both, *allowing* bargain-ing and compromise among different political forces for the resolution of social conflicts, *institutionalizing* the pluralist structures and procedures by which different political forces are allowed to compete over the power, *reg-ularizing* transfer of power, and *engaging* in the fundamental transformation of political structure.

Implicit in this definition is that a transition starts when the authoritarian regime begins to liberalize and that the transitional phase is complete once the first free, open and fair national election is held.[1] O'Donnell and Schmitter (1986), argue that "the typical sign that the transition has begun comes when … authoritarian incumbents, for whatever reason, begin to modify their own rules in the direction of providing more secure guarantees for the rights of individuals and groups" (6). Przeworski (1991) suggests that "Liberalization is a result of an interaction between splits in the authoritarian regime and autonomous organization of the civil society" (57). In this period, incumbent authoritarian rulers extend a measure of civil and political rights to individuals and groups (Sørensen 1993, 43). Space for oppositional political activity is created within a framework controlled by the autocratic regime. Liberalization is "the process of making effective certain rights that protect both individuals and social groups from arbitrary or illegal acts committed by the state or third parties" (O'Donnell and Schmitter 1986, 7).

An opening in the authoritarian regime often occurs through negotiation between hard-line and soft-line factions (35). Hardliners commit to the idea that the regime should continue indefinitely in its current state, possibly out of opportunism or fear that democracy would bring disaster to the nation (Farcau 1996, 41), and themselves. Softliners, or reform-minded people, believe that political freedom must be created in order to provide legitimacy to the regime and thereby sustain its power over the long run.

Transitions occur from above (elite-driven) or below (mass-driven) or in combination, which presents three patterns or modes of transition. For example, transitions can consist of bargaining and compromise among a select set of elite actors; however, transitions sometimes involve mass uprising and violent overthrow of the authoritarian regime, especially when the dictatorship is unwilling to engage in talks with the opposition. Hungary represents an example of a transition from above, where the transition emerged from divisions within the communist elite, while East Germany highlights a transition from below where hundreds of thousands of protestors took to the streets in Leipzig demanding an end to dictatorship. Whereas the starting point of the democratic transition consists of liberalization of the *ancien regime*, the goal of a transition is democracy, signified by free and fair national elections and a steady progression towards consolidation.

Measuring the end date of a transition by a competitive national election is relatively easy; measuring the start date is not; however, it is possible to pinpoint when liberalization has begun only through qualitative historical analysis. Liberalization is a controlled partial opening of the political space, or only a limited and controlled concession of political and civil rights from above, releasing political prisoners, opening up some issues for public debate, loosening censorship, and the like, but short of choosing a government through free, open, and competitive elections. Liberalization, like transition, may be a long drawn out process or may be reverted as quickly as it starts. In the ideal setting, liberalization sets the ground work for the process of transition and democratization to start. However, it does not necessarily lead to democratic transition.

We search for a *trigger event* to determine when the process of democratization starts. This is a reasonable approach and consistent with the literature. Colomer (2000) argues that the process of regime change is usually triggered by some critical event (11) which is usually signified by a visible split in the regime or popular mobilization (see, for example, Przeworski 1991). In coding our cases (which are discussed in greater detail in Chapter 4) we determine the trigger event that started the process of democratization. For example, the death of a dictator may create a democratic opening in long-standing personalistic regimes or military defeat may undermine the ruling elite and start the process of liberalization (e.g., Argentina 1983). Alternatively, increased protests by opposition groups may force a weakened incumbent regime into transitional talks that result in concessions that lead the country towards democracy (e.g., South Korea mid-1980s and East Germany 1990). In considering trigger events, it is important to note that they usually consist of a series of events rather than a single event; however, the series of events are dependent upon each other.

To demonstrate a trigger event, we provide a brief overview of Taiwan's and Romania's transition in the late twentieth century. On December 21, 1991 the first nationwide competitive elections were held since the Nationalist Party, or Kuomintang (KMT), retreated to Taiwan in 1949, marking the end point of the democratic transition. Yet, when did the transition start and what was the critical event that paved the way for democratization? In Taiwan, the transition commenced in 1986 when President Chiang Ching-kuo started to liberalize the political system. Two key events signaled the start of reform: in March of 1986 at a meeting of the KMT, the Third Central Committee, Chiang announced his intention to open up the political system; then the opposition formed the Democratic Progressive Party (DPP) on September 28. Despite the DPP's illegal status under martial law and the eagerness of many KMT leaders to squash the DPP, Chiang allowed the party to remain. Then in 1987, after 38 years of martial law, Chiang lifted the restriction paving the way for liberalization and eventual democratization. The first significant opening in Taiwan is traced back to Chiang's tolerance of opposition parties. Had he prohibited their existence, Taiwan would have continued along an authoritarian path. The allowance of opposition parties signaled that the political order was changing and also provided legitimacy to previously forbidden parties. Allowing opposition parties also implied that they could compete in politics, a path the DDP would vigorously pursue. Liberalization of the system continued with the lifting of martial law, closely monitored and led by the incumbent regime. Thus, Taiwan characterizes an incumbent-led transition.

In Romania, the trigger event to democratization occurred in December of 1989 as the hard-line regime of Nicolae Ceauşescu attempted to forcibly remove the popular dissident Hungarian reformist pastor László Tőkés in the western city of Timişoara. Protestors attempted to halt the removal of Tőkés who had recently made critical comments toward the Ceauşescu regime in the international media, and the government alleged he was inciting ethnic hatred. At the behest of the government, the bishop of Timişoara removed Tőkés from his post, thereby depriving him of the right to use the apartment he was entitled to as a pastor. For some time, parishioners gathered around his home to protect him from harassment and eviction. Many passers-by, including religious Romanian students, unaware of the details and having been told by the pastor's supporters that this was yet another attempt by the Ceauşescu regime to restrict religious freedom, spontaneously joined in. However, the protests grew and quickly swelled into massive anti-government protests against the policies of Ceauşescu – students, workers, men and women descended upon the old city's Opera Square.

Losing site of the original purpose of the gathering, but aware of the events sweeping across Eastern Europe threatening long-standing totalitarian communist regimes, the Romanian protests in Timişoara quickly lost the connection to their initial cause and transformed into general anti-government demonstrations. The demonstrations continued into the following days and on Monday, December 17, the army fired into the crowd on the order of Ceauşescu, killing around 70 people between December 16 and 22. Immediately following the armed forces intervention, tens of thousands of industrial workers in Timişoara peacefully took up protests on the 18th; by the 20th the city was in insurrection. Ceauşescu, on December 21, still believing he was firmly in charge of his country, was in the midst of a carefully planned speech to an assembly of working people from Bucharest. He spoke from the balcony of the Central Committee building of the Communist Party Headquarters in an effort to rally support for his government in the wake of turbulent events shaking Eastern Europe at the time.

Ceauşescu would use the event to reassert his control over Romania, the country he had ruled absolutely since 1965. In a matter of seconds, it all changed. The chants of Timişoara quickly turned to *'Death, Death,'* in open reference to Ceauşescu himself, unprecedented and unbelievable to the dictator and his protectorates. Resorting to past control tactics, he gestured for silence to the crowd when he had grown weary of their applause. It had no effect. Ceauşescu glanced anxiously to his wife Elena and to other dignitaries on the balcony, his bewilderment obvious. For the first time in his repressive regime, he had lost control and knew it, yet by the look on his face he could not believe it. The chief of his personal security detail whisked him inside the building, and television transmission was cut and replaced by martial music.[2] Quickly thereafter he and Elena fled with some core supporters; within the next four days they would be captured, tried and executed by firing squad on Christmas day. Free elections occurred in Romania just six months later. The transition in Romania was led by a powerful opposition to the incumbent regime, most notably through popular uprising from below (commonly referred to as a "revolution").

The events in Taiwan and Romania demonstrate that the time lag varies tremendously among transition types. The sudden overthrow of Ceauşescu would lead to democratic elections within months, while the interval between the start of liberalization in Taiwan and the first free election exceeded five years. In both cases, as in all transitions, a series of events are identifiable that starts a snowballing effect of democratization; that once these events occur, there is little, if anything, that can reverse the course of action set in motion. For each country examined in this study, we search for that defining event to understand how regime change was initiated to facilitate coding the mode of transition from dictatorship to democracy.

Transitional processes are also distinguished by whether they are peaceful or violent. Negotiated transitions, such as Taiwan and South Korea, are peaceful and often protracted; liberalization by an incumbent regime rarely leads to immediate national elections but proceeds incrementally. Violent transitions in contrast, frequently occur abruptly, but not always. After Ceauşescu's fall, a provisional government, formed by a group of communists led by Ion Iliescu of the National Salvation Front, assumed power. On May 20, 1990, the National Salvation Front won the national elections and Ion Iliescu, who had taken power after Ceauşescu's execution, remained president. Romania's transition lasted approximately six months. The Romanians' struggle to deepen their democracy, however, continues.

Transitional modes

There is a large literature on the modes of transition from authoritarianism to democracy. Scholars categorize democratizing states into varying modes of transition, for the purpose of classifying historic and contemporary cases (see, for example, Dahl 1971; Linz 1978; Linz 1981; Share 1984; Share and Mainwaring 1986; Share 1987; Linz 1990; Karl 1990; Huntington 1991; Karl and Schmitter 1991; Munck and Leff 1997). The classification of different modes of transition is used to examine their effects on democratic deepening (Dahl 1971; Huntington 1984; Karl 1990; Huntington 1991), the diverse problems and trade-offs faced during the transition and consolidation periods (O'Donnell 1989, 1992; Valenzuela 1992), and the causal link between transition type and the kind of democracy that follows (Linz 1981). The prior works on transition type are based on case studies and regional analyses.[3] The point of departure of this study from the existing literature is to examine democratic transitions cross-nationally through quantitative analysis, rather than through qualitative regional and case study approaches.

To proceed, we devised four transitional modes to reflect the nature and characteristics of the democratization process that includes the balance of power between incumbents and elites. Important as the basis of a comprehensive statistical analysis is to create modes that are generalizable enough to categorize all transitioning states and reflect the trigger event that allows us to place them into a specific category. While there are various studies that put forth transitional modes, we find them somewhat unsatisfying because they are limited in scope and created by examining particular regions and/or countries. On the other hand, they provide a solid foundation from which to expand upon. Our goal, therefore, is to devise broader categories so that any state can be placed into its appropriate transition type. To justify theoretically why this is a superior approach to classifying transitioning states, consider the issue of pacts in transitions. While many transitions are characterized by negotiations between incumbents and opposition groups, we view pacts as a subset of converted and cooperative transitions. Taiwan's transition was largely incumbent led and the opposition was too weak to impose demands on the powerful ruling KMT. However, viewing pacts as a subset of negotiated transitions not only allows us to place pure incumbent-led transitions in the conversion category but also those where opposition groups played a more active role in the process. We believe the trade-off of generalization to specificity is minor because all converted transitions imply that incumbents are more powerful than the opposition; yet, a certain level of variation exists and we account for this in the categorization. For purposes of classification, we develop the following categories, and provide a prototype for each transition type.

Conversion

(1) *Conversion* – when the elites in power take the lead in democratization and the government is stronger than the opposition. The incumbent elites seek reform, and lead the reform process. Sometimes a faction of the ruling elite prompts an opening to reform from above, or elites agree upon a multilateral compromise. In certain cases, incumbents transition (or convert) the state with no input from opposition groups; however, opposition groups often play some role in the transition even though they are weaker than incumbents. As a result, *incumbent-led negotiated pacts* can be viewed as a sub-category of regime conversion. Examples of countries that have transitioned to democracy by conversion include Taiwan, the U.S.S.R., Bulgaria and Chile. Similar categorizations by other scholars are *Transformation* (Huntington); *Transaction* (Share/Mainwaring); *Reforma* (Linz); *Pact* (Karl and Schmitter); and *Reform through Extrication/Revolution from Above* (Munck and Leff).

Taiwan is an example of transition by conversion. In the mid-1980s, President Chiang Ching-kuo initiated a series of liberalizing reforms, including the toleration of opposition parties. After lifting martial law in the summer of 1987, Chiang died suddenly of a heart attack in January of 1988. His hand-picked successor, Lee Teng-hui, succeeded to the presidency and KMT chairmanship. President Lee, like Chiang, was committed to reform and shared the late president's vision. A native Taiwanese, Lee broadened the support of the KMT by bringing more Taiwanese into the cabinet and Central Standing Committee. As a result, the ethnic balance of power began to shift from the mainlanders to the Taiwanese. Under Lee, Taiwan steadily moved towards a democratic political system. Significant measures of political liberalization under Lee included the mandatory retirement in 1991 of "senior representatives" of the national parliamentary bodies elected from mainland constituencies in 1947 and the first legislative elections, held on December 21, 1991; the KMT won the majority of the vote. Constitutional reform provided for the popular election of the president and vice-president beginning in 1996, in which Lee won 54 percent of the vote. During the liberalization process, the KMT shaped the reform process without much consultation or input from opposition groups.

(2) *Cooperative* – democratization is the result of joint action by government and opposition groups. Change occurs inside and outside the incumbent elite and reforms occur through cooperation between incumbents and opposition groups. Within the government, there is a balance between reformers and standpatters such that the government is willing to negotiate a change of regime (Huntington 1991, 151). Viewing regime cooperation as an *opposition-led negotiated pact* reflects the advantage of the opposition. Among the countries that have had a cooperative transition are Poland, Czechoslovakia, Hungary, Nicaragua, South Korea, and Bolivia. Other scholars classify these as *Transplacement* (Huntington); *Extrication* (Share/Mainwaring); *Reform through Transaction* (Munck and Leff); *Pact* (Karl and Schmitter);[4] and *Reform from below* (Munck and Leff).

South Korea's transition to democracy is an example of a cooperative process. During the Fifth Republic (1979 to 1987) Chun Doo-hwan, a military colleague of the late president Park Chung-hee, controlled the government. The Fifth Republic attempted extensive efforts at reform, which resulted from a vocal civil society that emerged after the assassination of Park. Protests were carried out mostly by university students and labor unions. On May 18, 1980, violence broke out in the city of Gwangju between students of Chonnam National University who were protesting the closure of the university and the armed forces. The students resisted the military for nine days. Estimates of the civilian death toll ranged from a few dozen to 2,000, with a full investigation later setting the count at 207. Public outrage over the killings consolidated nationwide support for democracy, forcing the government to grant several concessions, including the restoration of direct presidential elections.

In 1987 Roh Tae-woo, a former general, was elected president (due to a split in the opposition), but additional democratic advances during his tenure resulted in the 1992 election of long-time pro-democracy activist, Kim Young-sam. Kim became South Korea's first civilian president in 32 years. The 1997 presidential election and peaceful transfer of power marked another step forward in South Korea's democratization when Kim Dae-jung, a life-long democracy and human rights activist, was elected from a major opposition party. During the transitional period, opposition groups influenced the change, as did incumbents who opted to bargain their way to democracy rather than face violent removal. Most importantly, opposition demands for democracy and reform were almost entirely agreed upon by the incumbents.

(3) *Collapse* – Opposition groups take the lead in bringing about democracy, and the authoritarian regime collapses or is overthrown. Collapse encompasses transition by revolution or coup d'état where the masses overthrow their rulers (Thompson 2006). The opposition dictates the transition with little or no control asserted by the incumbent elite, who are too weak to control the process, such as when the masses rise up in arms and overthrow the government through violence. Democratic reformers are notably weak in or absent from the regime and incumbents refuse to negotiate a transfer of power. Incumbents may believe that

they have a distinct power advantage over the opposition; therefore they refuse to engage in talks. Alternatively, the opposition senses growing support among the masses, and frustrated by the absence of reform, forces a transition through conflict. Regime collapse has occurred in East Germany, Romania, Greece, Portugal, and Argentina. Other scholars refer to collapse as *Replacement* (Huntington); *Ruptura* (Linz); *Breakdown/Collapse* (Share/Mainwaring); *Revolution/ Imposition* (Karl and Schmitter); and *Reform through Rupture* (Munck and Leff).

On February 7, 1986 President Ferdinand Marcos, who had ruled the Philippines for 20 years, ran for re-election against Corazon Aquino, widow of slain opposition leader Benigno Aquino. Marcos had Parliament declare him the winner, even though Aquino actually won more votes. Mass demonstrations ensued and two prominent generals and Marco supporters, Enrile and Ramos, announced to the nation they were breaking away from the Marcos camp and supporting Aquino. When Marcos learned about the defection of Enrile and Ramos, he immediately went on nationwide radio and TV to announce that he had discovered and foiled a plot to overthrow the government and demanded that Ramos and Enrile surrender. Sensing growing frustration and a loss of popular support, he promised to look into the grievances of the reformists; however, it was too late, similar to Ceauşescu's last minute desperate promises to increase wages and pension benefits on the eve of the Romanian revolution. Nationwide protests ensued and rather than be forced from power, or worse, Marcos fled to Hawaii for exile on February 25, 1986. Aquino was then sworn in as president. In the Philippines, Marcos refused to reform the system of government or negotiate with the opposition until he had lost the support of the military. Protests led to his quick political demise and the installation of a democratically elected leader. More recently, both Egypt (2011) and Libya (2011) have experienced a change in the political order through collapse.

(4) *Foreign Intervention* – foreign military interference is used to remove the authoritarian regime and occurs when a dominant external power topples the *ancien régime*. Interventions by foreign military invaders share many of the same traits as replacement: incumbent reformers are virtually non-existent and the current regime is opposed to change, as evident in Iraq under Saddam Hussein. Foreign intervention has been used in countries such as Grenada, Panama, Afghanistan and Iraq, and similarly referred to by other scholars as *Intervention* (Huntington); and *Imposition* (Karl and Schmitter).

Saddam Hussein's regime held a tight grip on power for over 30 years. No opposition groups or dissent was tolerated and the populace was closely monitored through an extensive "neighborhood watch" program; thus there was no domestic group capable of removing him from power. Change could only occur through external force: in this case a coalition led by the United States. As in the case of regime collapse, rulers who are forcibly removed from power often face death, exile or incarceration (e.g., Hussein who was executed, or Noriega from Panama, who has been incarcerated since his removal from power in 1990).

Democratic consolidation

The third and final step of democratization is sustainability, or consolidation. Once states transition to democracy, how do they stay and become more democratic? Consolidation extends beyond procedural minimalist definition of democracy as laid out by Huntington (1991) and expanded by Dahl (1971). Transitioning states do not transform themselves from dictatorships to consolidated democracies overnight. If the transition culminates in a competitive election, then the procedural, minimal definition of democracy can distinguish a newly democratic regime from its authoritarian predecessor; however, this does not equate to democratic consolidation.

Consolidation suggests that knowing that no matter what challenges lay ahead, elites and masses believe that democracy is the best form of government to solve problems. Consolidation means that democratic institutions and practices are firmly ingrained in the political culture and result in increases in political equality. While numerous states make the transition from authoritarianism to democracy on the minimalist criterion of free elections, the process of embedding the democracy in a society is, to say the least, difficult.

Numerous scholars have offered definitions of consolidation. Diamond (1999) explains consolidation as a "broad and deep legitimation, such that all significant political actors, at both the elite and mass levels, believe that the democratic regime is the most right and appropriate for their society, better than any other realistic alternative they can image" (65). Linz and Stepan offer an influential conceptual framework of consolidation through which "democracy becomes routinized and deeply internalized in social, institutional, and even psychological life, as well as in political calculations for achieving success" (16). While Linz and Stepan argue that conflict may persist in democratic societies, no significant political or social actors attempt to subvert the process and achieve their objectives through illegal means. Dahl (1997) claims that democracy implies and requires "a strong democratic culture that provides adequate emotional and cognitive support for adhering to democratic procedures" (34). Rudra (2005) argues that consolidation "requires that a significant majority chooses political leaders in free, uncorrupt elections, and it means that the previously disenfranchised have an increasing influence in determining political decisions particularly with respect to redistribution" (707). Whether the parameters of democratic consolidation include "broad and deep legitimation" or "adhering to democratic procedures," it must comprise some more profound change in social value and norm beyond the procedural and institutional requirements.

Democratic consolidation is a discernible process by which democratic values, norms and principles are firmly entrenched within society, such that political and social actors, both elites and the masses believe that democracy is "the only game in town," the only legitimate framework recognized and accepted by all major political forces to seek and exercise political power, and through which democracy becomes standardized and internalized in institutional, social and cultural life. In a consolidated democracy, there may be intense conflicts, but no significant political actors attempt to achieve their objectives by illegal, unconstitutional, or antidemocratic means.

Despite urgent problems and intense conflict, when not only political leaders but the vast majority of political actors look to democracy to solve their problems, democracy is consolidated. Key to this definition is that rather than subversion of democracy when any group's desired outcome is not obtained, the promise of future elections curbs the need for violence. In this regard, democracy assumes its place as the right and natural political order. The danger, of course, is that in newly democratized states, the citizenry is unconvinced of the merits of democracy. For example, assume that Country A experienced rapid and steady economic growth under a dictatorship. Then, a transition occurs and the economy cools off, after a peaceful transfer of power to a new opposition leader. Unemployment and inflation rise. Without a democratic tradition, the citizens may believe that a return to dictatorship is a better way to stimulate the economy than voting the new government out of office and replacing it with one with better growth policies. Where democracy is relatively unknown, it must prove itself.

Advancing the debate

The contradictory descriptions of regime transition modes on the prospects for democratic consolidation leave more questions than answers, due to lack of empirical analysis and conceptual imprecision. The literature is largely based on regional and country-specific studies which limit their generalizability; cross-national statistical analyses are an important next step to determine whether transition types matter. Further, the differing approaches to transitions are rooted in structuralist, strategic choice, institutional, or political economy approaches, often to the exclusivity of one over the other. According to Guo (1999) "...these theoretical approaches fits the observed facts to some extent but none of them provides an adequate explanation if applied to particular cases" (144); rather "In the reality of transition, some of the causal factors are structural, some institutional, some political economic and others ... mixed" (144). Our goal is to synthesize these approaches into an analytical framework that offers a finer approach to understanding the consequences and legacies of transitions. For example, several studies base the success or failure of democracy on the adoption of certain electoral rules (see, for example, Lijphart 1990, 1999; Powell 2000; McDonald and Budge 2005). While this is an integral part of the story, we must also understand the actors that make the choices and why they make them. Here, strategic choice among elites leads to institutional design in the new democracy. Rather than elite preferences and institutions constituting mutually exclusive characters in our story, together they interact to provide a more complete picture of why democratic transitions matter.

In this chapter, we have shown that regime transitions occur through a variety of ways and are categorized in terms of conversion, cooperation, collapse and foreign intervention. Further, the consensus in the literature is that the mode of transition directly affects the prospects for democratic consolidation – that some modes are more likely to lead to democratic deepening than others and it is possible to conceptualize and measure democratic quality and duration and empirically test it against any given mode of transition. In the next chapter, we develop a theory of transitions in order to explain why they are relevant to democratic success.

Notes

1 By "complete" we do not mean consolidated. Consolidation is a lengthy process and is even more difficult to measure than democratic transitions.
2 Martial music, also known as martial industrial, is a music genre originating in late twentieth century Europe. It borrows musically from classical, neofolk and neoclassical music, and traditional European marches.
3 Huntington's (1991) *The Third Wave* is one of the few scholarly works on transitions that assumes a cross-national approach although it is not quantitative.
4 When Karl and Schmitter discuss *Pact*, they do not distinguish elites in power from elite reformers, hence the overlap.

References

Burkhart, Ross E. and Michael S. Lewis-Beck. 1994. "Comparative Democracy: The Economic Development Thesis." *The American Political Science Review* 88(4): 903–910.

Colomer, Josep M. 2000. *Strategic Transitions: Game Theory and Democratization.* Baltimore: The Johns Hopkins University Press.

Cutright, Philips. 1963. "National Political Development: Measurement and Analysis." *American Sociological Review* 28: 253–264.

Dahl, Robert A. 1971. *Polyarchy: Participation and Opposition.* New Haven: Yale University Press.

Dahl, Robert A. 1997. "Development and Democratic Culture." In *Consolidating the Third Wave Democracies; Themes and Perspectives*, ed. Larry Diamond, Marc F. Plattner, Yun-han Chu and Hung-mao Tien. Baltimore: Johns Hopkins University Press, 34–39.

Diamond, Larry. 1999. *Developing Democracy: Toward Consolidation.* Baltimore: Johns Hopkins University Press.

Di Palma, Giuseppe. 1990. *To Craft Democracies.* Berkeley: University of California Press.

Epstein, David L., Robert Bates, Jack Goldstone, Ida Kristensen and Sharyn O'Halloran. 2006. "Democratic Transitions." *American Journal of Political Science* 50(3): 551–569.

Farcau, Bruce W. 1996. *The Transition to Democracy in Latin America: The Role of the Military.* Westport: Praeger.

Gill, Graeme. 2000. *The Dynamics of Democratization: Elites, Civil Society and the Transition Process.* New York: St. Martin's Press.

Guo, Sujian. 1999. "Democratic Transition: A Critical Overview." *Issues & Studies* 35(4): 133–148.

Huntington, Samuel P. 1984. "Will More Countries Become Democratic?" *Political Science Quarterly* 99: 195–198.

Huntington, Samuel P. 1991. *The Third Wave: Democratization in the Late Twentieth Century.* Norman: University of Oklahoma Press.

Jackman, Robert W. 1973. "On the Relation of Economic Development to Democratic Performance." *American Journal of Political Science* 17(3): 611–621.

Karl, Terry Lynn. 1990. "Dilemmas of Democratization in Latin America." *Comparative Politics* 23(1): 1–21.

Karl, Terry Lynn and Philippe C. Schmitter. 1991. "Modes of transition in Latin America, Southern and Eastern Europe." *International Social Science Journal* 128: 269–284.

Kitschelt, Herbert. 1992. "Political Regime Change: Structure and Process-Driven Explanations?" *American Political Science Review* 86(4): 1032.

Laothamatas, Anek. 1997. *Democratization in Southeast and East Asia.* Singapore: Institute of Southeast Asian Studies.

Lijphart, Arend. 1990. "The Political Consequences of Electoral Laws, 1945–85." *Amercian Political Science Review* 84: 481–496.

Lijphart, Arend. 1999. *Patterns of Democracy: Government Forms and Performance in Thirty-Six Countries.* New Haven: Yale University Press.

Linz, Juan. 1978. "Crisis Breakdown and Reequilibration." In *The Breakdown of Democratic Regimes*, ed. Juan J. Linz and Alfred Stepan. Baltimore and London: The Johns Hopkins University Press.

Linz, Juan. 1981. "Some Comparative Thoughts on the Transition to Democracy in Portugal and Spain." In *Portugal since the Revolution: Economic and Political Perspectives*, ed. Jorge Braga de Macedo and Simon Serfaty. Boulder: Westview Press.

Linz, Juan. 1990. **(a or b)?** "The Perils of Presidentialism." *Journal of Democracy* (Winter): 51:69.

Linz, Juan. 1990. **(a or b)?** "Transitions to Democracy." *The Washington Quarterly* (Summer): 143–164.

Linz, Juan and Alfred Stepan, eds. 1978 *The Breakdown of Democratic Regimes.* Baltimore: Johns Hopkins University Press.

Linz, Juan and Alfred Stepan. 1996. *Problems of Democratic Transition and Consolidation: Southern Europe, South America and Post-Communist Europe.* Baltimore: The Johns Hopkins University Press.

Lipset, Seymour Martin. 1959. "Some Social Requisites of Democracy: Economic Development and Political Legitimacy." *American Political Science Review* 5: 69–105.

Londregan, John B. and Keith T. Poole. 1996. "Does High Income Promote Democracy?" *World Politics* 49: 1–30.

Marx, Karl and Frederick Engels. 1848. *Manifesto of the Communist Party.* New York: International Publishers 100th Anniversary Edition.

McDonald, Michael D. and Budge, Ian. 2005. *Elections, Parties, Democracy: Conferring the Median Mandate.* Oxford: Oxford University Press.

Moore, Barrington, Jr. 1966. *Social Origins of Dictatorship and Democracy.* Boston: Beacon Press.

Munck, Gerardo L. and Carol Skalnik Leff. 1997. "Modes of Transition and Democratization: South American and Eastern Europe in Comparative Perspective." *Comparative Politics* 29: 343–362.

O'Donnell, Guillermo. 1989. "Transitions to Democracy: Some Navigation Instruments." In *Democracy in the Americas: Stopping the Pendulum*, ed. Robert A. Pastor. New York and London: Holmes and Meier: 87–104.

O'Donnell, Guillermo. 1992. "Transitions, Continuities, and Paradoxes." In *Issues in Democratic Consolidation: The New South American Democracies in Comparative Perspective*, ed. Scott Mainwaring, Guillermo O'Donnell and J. Samuel Valenzuela. Notre Dame: Notre Dame Press: 17–56.

O'Donnell, Guillermo and Phillippe Schmitter. 1986. *Transitions from Authoritarian Rule: Tentative Conclusions about Uncertain Democracies*. Baltimore: The Johns Hopkins University Press.

Philip, George. 2003. *Democracy in Latin America.* Cambridge: Polity Press.

Powell G. Bingham. (2000) *Elections as Instruments of Democracy: Majoritarian and Proportional Visions*. New Haven: Yale University Press.

Przeworski, Adam. 1991. *Democracy and the Market.* New York: Cambridge University Press.

Przeworski, Adam and Fernando Limongi. 1997. "Modernization: Theories and Facts." *World Politics* 49: 155–183.

Przeworski, Adam, Michael Alvarez, Jose Antonio Cheibub and Fernando Limongi. 2000. *Democracy and Development: Political Institutions and Well-Being in the World, 1950–1990*. New York: Cambridge University Press.

Rudra, Nita. 2005. "Globalization and the Strengthening of Democracy in the Developing World." *American Journal of Political Science* 49(4): 704–730.

Rueschemeyer, Dietrich, John Stepens and Evelyne Huber Stephens. 1992. *Capitalist Development and Democracy*. Chicago: University of Chicago Press.

Share, Donald. 1984. "Transition through Transaction: The Politics of Democratization in Spain, 1975–1977." Ph.D. dissertation. Stanford University.

Share, Donald. 1987. "Transitions to Democracy and Transition through Transaction." *Comparative Political Studies* 19: 525–548.

Share, Donald and Scott Mainwaring. 1986. "Transitions through transaction: democratization in Brazil and Spain." In *Political Liberalization in Brazil: Dynamics, Dilemmas and Future Prospects*, ed. Wayne Selcher. Boulder: Westview, 175–215.

Sørensen, Georg. 1993. *Democracy and Democratization*. Boulder: Westview Press.

Thompson, Mark R. 2006. *Democratic Revolutions Asia and Eastern Europe*. London: Routledge.

Valenzuela, Samuel J. 1992. "Democratic Consolidation in Post-Transitional Settings: Notion, Process, and Facilitating Conditions." In *Issues in Democratic Consolidation: The New South American Democracies in Comparative* Perspective, ed. Scott Mainwaring, Guillermo O'donnell and J. Samuel Valenzuela. Notre Dame: University of Notre Dame Press: 57–104.

Wright, Joseph. 2006. "Political Competition and Democratic Stability in New Democracies." *British Journal of Political Science* 38: 221–245.

3   A theory of explaining the success rate of democratic transitions

To understand why democratic outcomes are influenced by the transitional process, it is necessary to advance a theory to explain the success rate of democratic transitions, i.e., which mode of transition will result in a higher percentage of success in maintaining democratic outcomes (higher survival rate) and quality of democracy (higher average level of democracy). Transitions are complex historical events and to fully understand them requires an exploration of the mechanisms at play among political elites during the transitional process. In doing so, we are able to link the specific events occurring within a transition, such as the relative power advantage among incumbents and opposition groups, and demonstrate how this leads to divergent outcomes; this is our theoretical point of departure from the existing literature. Thus, for transitions to have any meaningful purpose they must help us better understand why democracy succeeds in some cases and fails in others. In a broader context, unpacking the mechanisms of democratic transitions provides us with the leverage necessary to determine the chances for sustainable democracy. Where circumstances are unfavorable, we can also then better understand how to hedge authoritarian reversion.

Violent and peaceful transitions

Regime transitions are the interval between one political regime and the next (O'Donnell and Schmitter 1986), with a democratic transition representing the interval between an authoritarian regime and a democratic regime. Within transitional types, two distinguishing features encompass all democratizing states: (1) the smoothness of the transition (whether it is peaceful or violent), and (2) the balance of power among incumbent elites and opposition groups, which in turn, (see Figure 3.1) determines whether the transition is inclusive or exclusive.

Negotiation characterizes peaceful transitions (cooperative transitions and converted transitions). In cooperative transitions, incumbent elites and opposition groups work together to transition the state, bargaining over such issues as the timing of elections, the adoption of electoral rules, the separation of the military from civilian politics, resolution of social conflict, and the pace and scope of economic reforms. The balance of power between incumbent and opposition groups is important in negotiated transitions – the party or individuals with the power advantage is inclined to design electoral rules to secure its place in the new democracy, as it seeks the greatest distributive payoff. Benoit and Schiemann (2001) argue "...in transitional contexts, political actors both can and do calculate and pursue self-interest when adopting political institutions" (154). In the regime-led mode of transition, i.e., conversion, the incumbents are in an advantageous position, and tend to lead and even dominate the peaceful transition process, which is often less inclusive in transforming the old regime and converting it to a democratic one.

Violent transitions (collapse and foreign intervention) reflect either a lack of, or breakdown in, negotiations with the incumbent regime and frequently involve bloodshed; the power disparities in these transitions are considerable. Unless a more powerful opposition can force a weak incumbent government to transition the state, that opposition will unite and initiate regime overthrow through violence (collapse or also known as *Revolution*). Here, incumbent rulers are unable to maintain their unchallenged domination and the opposition seeks to eliminate them through armed conflict in order to implement their preferred regime alternative. When a dominant incumbent regime is unwilling to negotiate a democratic transition, the only means of removing it is through foreign intervention. In the twentieth century, this has typically taken the form of military intervention by the United States. Transition by regime collapse and foreign intervention is generally violent and defined by intense power struggles between intransigent hardliners and opposition groups insisting on a new system of governance. Within violent transitions, it is difficult to determine how inclusionary they are and we discuss this in detail below.

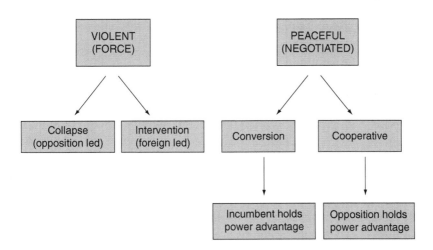

Figure 3.1 Classifying transitions.

Institutions

Regardless of whether regime transformation is peaceful or violent, democratic transitions are associated with profound institutional change. In the new democracy, the institutions imposed by authoritarian regimes, including the constitution and electoral system, must be redesigned (Saxer 2003). From the transition emerges the institutions that define the rules of the new democratic game, and the nature of the transition determines who possesses the greatest power advantage, and therefore makes the rules. According to Geddes (1996) "…transitions are periods of great political ferment and creativity and are a time for political soul-searching about the causes of previous democratic breakdowns" (30). The drafting of new constitutions and electoral rules (i.e., the method of translating votes into seats) by the actors involved in creating the new democracy is one of the major institutional assignments of transition players. To Przeworski (1991), "solutions to the problem of democratization consist of institutions" (39). Lijphart argues (1992) that *the* most important constitutional choices in new democracies are those of the electoral system – either majoritarian or proportional representation (207). The adoption of a particular electoral system has important consequences. For example, there is no doubt that electoral systems significantly influence the number of parties in a society (Duverger 1954) with "the simple-majority single-ballot system favor[ing] the two-party system" and "the simple-majority rule with two ballots and proportional representation favor[ing] multipartyism" (217–239). What are the potential implications? Where multiple opposition groups exist, but are collectively less powerful than incumbents who favor a simple-majority ballot system, they will feel excluded under a two-party system. In this scenario, electoral rules may lead to the exclusion of opposition parties and this is not favorable to the new democracy. Excluded opposition parties may seek alternative means of affecting change. As noted by Przeworski (1991) "the democratic institutions … systematically generate outcomes that cause some politically important forces to subvert them" (37). Depending on the degree of subversion, excluded forces may turn to violence to generate a more favorable outcome.

Fortifying democracy, in theory, should be the main consideration of institutional drafters; yet, at the same time, actors are concerned with positioning themselves and their parties for the most advantageous place in the government, supporting electoral laws that they believe are "best for them" (Andrews and Jackman 2005, 68). Geddes (1996) states, "As parties began to negotiate new institutional arrangements, each [seeks] choices that would give it an advantage over the competition or, at a minimum, ensure survival" (21). That is, transitional players seek to maximize their power under the new system of government, whether by achieving a majority in the parliament or capturing the presidency and crafting institutions (i.e., electoral rules) that benefit them the most. Yet, in many instances the initial state of the regime transition includes a significant crisis of the autocratic regime and actors may be unsure of their relative strength and therefore make decisions on the basis of expectations, promises and threats (Colomer 2000, 30). O'Donnell and Schmitter (1986) note "In founding elections after a period of more or less protracted authoritarian rule ... uncertainty of outcomes is particularly high"(61). For example, voters will have little if no experience in choosing among candidates; party identification will be weak and candidate image unclear – all of the items people in mature democracies rely upon to make decisions. Further, voters may simply be suspicious and untrusting of the process. All of this leads to much uncertainty and poses challenges in the immediate posttransitional phase.

Bueno de Mesquita *et al.* (2003) argue the essence of politics is survival in office. "The desire to survive motivates the selection of policies and the allocation of benefits; it shapes the selection of political institutions and the objectives of foreign policies; it influences the very evolution of political life" (8–9). Key actors are likely to leverage their power for maximum benefit under the new system, either electoral success and/or policy outcomes; however, uncertainty also influences transitional outcomes. According to Geddes (1996), "...the members of roundtables, constituent assemblies, and legislatures who make the choices that determine electoral procedures – pursue their own individual interests above all else, and their interests center on furthering their political careers" (18). During negotiated transitions, for example, one side (either opposition or incumbents) holds the upper hand. In these transitions, it is the actors with the power advantage that exert the most influence in the bargaining process away from autocracy. However, Andrews and Jackman (2005) note that "uncertainty made it impossible for any political actor to predict how electoral design would affect party support" (68). Therefore, even though one group holds the power advantage and will use it to manipulate their desired outcome, uncertainty makes it impossible to predict the outcome with accuracy.

In discussing transitions, Sørensen (1993) notes, "Probably the most important factor influencing the outcome of the decision phase is the makeup of the leading coalition behind the transition" (44). This has profound consequences on both the rules and the durability of the new democracy. The ultimate pay-off for positioning actors is victory in a democratic election and the power to further define the new governmental structure and formulate its policies. According to Colomer (2000), two phases are distinguishable in the transitional process regarding institutional choice (109). First, there are the actors bargaining the transition after the process of liberalization has begun to shape pre-electoral arrangements. Next, constitutional arrangements proceed after the first round of elections, shaped by the relative strength of the transitional players. In phase one, actor strength is more perceived than tangible (e.g., incumbents are more powerful because the armed forces stand behind them); in phase two, after the first election, actor strength becomes more tangible through electoral performance. Thus, it is important to understand who the relevant actors are in the pre-electoral process of change and the relative strength and weakness of the incumbent rulers and opposition in bargaining the outcomes.

Inclusionary and exclusionary mechanisms – the key to success

The bifurcation of transitions as either peaceful or violent has implications for the likelihood of war and the success of democracy (Ward and Gleditsch 1998; Wright 2006). Ward and Gleditsch (1998) show how smooth transitions toward democracy are associated with lower risks of war, while violent transitions are associated with increases in the likelihood of war. They note that "a possibly rocky process of democratization or transition towards a fragile democracy need not necessarily imply that countries become immediately more peaceful" (53). The implication is significant in that new democracies engaging in conflict are less likely to survive (Wright 2006). Conversely, smooth monotonic transitions are associated with the lowest risk of war and greatest benefit (59). As confirmed by Peter Ackerman (2007), Chairman of Freedom House,

> When less violence was used by the opposition more freedom followed ... there was more than a three to one chance that a country in transition would attain a high freedom rating post-transition if the opposition to dictatorship did not employ violent force.[1]

According to these arguments, smooth transitions should result in higher levels of democracy during the posttransitional phase than violent transitions because they are associated with a lower risk of war. This provides for a parsimonious yet unsatisfying theory. While we agree that violent transitions complicate the democratization process, the key to successful democratization is a result of whether or not the new system is inclusionary or exclusionary and both violent and peaceful transitions can contain inclusive or exclusive mechanisms. Inclusive regimes will survive for obvious reasons, most notably they offer a voice in government to both incumbent and opposition groups while exclusive regimes would appear to not be much better than their authoritarian predecessors. Even if an opposition group with democratic intentions emerges as the most powerful player in a violent transition and then attempts to exclude other groups in the process (in particular other democratic oriented groups) then monopolizing the system is unlikely to lead to a successful democracy.

To further develop this theory, we examine in greater detail each mode of transition and its inclusionary features, or lack thereof. Our goal is to demonstrate that regardless of transition type, *inclusive* transitions will be more likely to succeed while *exclusive* transitions will be more likely to fail. Certain transitions, cooperative in particular, are the most inclusive. Converted transitions, on the other hand, are the least inclusive. Violent transitions are more difficult to flesh out yet there are compelling reasons to suggest that foreign interventions are more inclusive than transition by collapse. The importance of whether a transition is inclusive or exclusive returns us to the importance of institutions and which parties are involved in drafting constitutions and determining electoral rules.

Violent transition by collapse and foreign intervention

By conventional wisdom, violent transitions reflect the harshness of the environment from which they emerge. According to Ward and Gleditsch (1998), "dangerous" transitions result in institutionalized states that resort to force during their revolutionary stage; the institutions and norms which emerge reflect this. They suggest that violent democratizations, such as those occurring through regime collapse, "...[are] often associated with increased likelihood of conflict and with possible subsequent escalation and war involvement" (53). While these regimes may be less repressive than their predecessors, they are also subject to instability and attempts by challengers to seize power (Ward and Gleditsch 1998, 53). Overthrowing a dictatorship and establishing a democracy typically means dismantling the prior system of government and starting anew.

Compared to peaceful transitions, violent transitions create greater uncertainty because they require a systemic effort in the creation and evolution of democratic institutions and the rule of law; however, an inclusive environment is likely to facilitate this. In regime collapse, we have seen examples of opposition groups uniting to remove the authoritarian polity but then fracturing afterwards in the struggle over the distribution of power and the creation of the new regime. In Nicaragua (1990), Iran (1979), Portugal (1973) and Romania (1990), the sudden collapse of authoritarian regimes led to struggles among previously non-unified opposition groups (Huntington 1991, 148) that had united to overthrow the government. During the conflict that ensued to remove the dictatorial regimes, the opposition groups contained inclusive elements by agreeing the best course of action was removal of the *ancien regime*. However, once that objective was achieved they became exclusionary and the group(s) with the power advantage exerted the most influence in dictating the terms and conditions of the new government; democracy was not always the outcome. In Nicaragua and Iran, for example, democratic moderates lost out; in Portugal, it was only after a protracted struggle between military factions, mass mobilization, demonstrations and strikes that a democratic course of governance emerged.

Throughout the twentieth century, most foreign interventions were carried out by the United States. Scholars define intervention as the direct or indirect use of military force for the purpose of "changing or preserving the structure of political authority in the target society" (Rosenau 1969, 161) and "a political use of military force involving ground troops of either the U.S. Army or Marine Corps in an active attempt to influence the behavior of other nations" (Blechman and Kaplan, 1978, 12). Some military interventions resemble revolutions, displaying great instability during the posttransitional stage, such as Haiti (1994), Afghanistan (2001) and Iraq (2003). In foreign interventions, opposition groups are not strong enough on their own to bring down the authoritarian regime; this is possible only through foreign invasion. As a consequence, the power struggle that erupts after the fall is often intense, leading to civil unrest and legitimacy problems.

There are exceptions. In Panama 1989–90, the United States restored a democratically elected regime by ousting the "election stealer" General Manuel

Noriega, who had ruled the country since 1983, and democracy proceeded smoothly. The U.S. military occupations of Japan, Germany, Austria and Italy after World War II led to major social, political, and economic reconstruction for the purpose of creating a democratic government. In many of these cases, however, democracy was simply restored to its pre-war levels. Further, the impending Cold War cannot be discounted as a factor in successful democratization. More recently, foreign interventions have led to differing results. In Haiti (1994), intervention by the United States resulted in civil unrest and the quick collapse of democratic rule. In Afghanistan (2001) and Iraq (2003), tribal and ethnic divisions plagued each country and the installed regimes suffer from legitimacy problems and were on the verge of collapse. Recent increase in U.S. military forces seems to be moving each country to a greater level of stability but democratic success is anything but certain at the time of this writing. The brutal dictatorships in Afghanistan and Iraq also decimated the system of government into a totalitarian police state leaving their successors the daunting challenge of rebuilding all institutions of government from the ground up.

Theoretically, there are compelling reasons why foreign intervention can be both favorable and unfavorable to democracy. On the favorable side, the intervening country, with its reputation at stake, provides large sums of financial support in the rebuilding of infrastructure (e.g., for 2009, the U.S. occupation of Iraq is estimated at US$7.3B per month, down from US$12B per month in 2008). Further, experienced democratic polities are in a position to offer political advice to liberated countries, help them set up a constitution and electoral system and arrange for an appropriate system of government that is inclusive of competing forces. Drawing on the resources of the democratic world, nations liberated through foreign intervention are in a unique position to access the varied resources of intergovernmental and non-governmental organizations as well (e.g., the United Nations, the World Bank, etc).

In ethnically and religiously diverse countries, years of repression of one group over another and the strife this caused is not always solved by liberation. Competing groups may refuse to work together in an inclusive environment in setting up their new government. Depending on how deep the divide runs between ethnically distinct groups it is possible that little can be accomplished without the ongoing presence of the foreign invader, and even then, the process of reconciliation can be both arduous and slow. This explains why democratic progress was swift in the homogenous societies of post-World War II Europe and more difficult in ethnically diverse countries. Yet, do not mistake this as supporting cultural arguments that suggest certain cultures are not conducive to democracy. It is not that ethnically diverse groups do not want democracy. Rather, they do not want to work together in achieving it (consider for example Yugoslavia and its breakup into five successor states which are now largely democratic). Transition by an occupational force may even include instances where political parties do not exist, "except in the minds of exiles or in the calculations of foreign powers" (O'Donnell and Schmitter 1986, 57). Further, the intentions of the occupying force and those internal groups that emerge as more powerful than others may only have limited liberalization as a goal with elections scheduled for an undefined future and for insignificant offices.

Peaceful transitions by conversion and cooperation

Peaceful transitions, characterized by compromise, are non-violent. The balance of power in these transitions is transparent and shapes and defines democratic rules. In peaceful cooperative transitions – *inclusiveness is key to success* – incumbent and opposition groups come together to negotiate the path towards democracy. Negotiated settlement allows both incumbents and opposition leaders or all major social forces to be involved in the democratic transition process, express preferences for democratic craftsmanship, tailor their demands accordingly, and integrate other social groups into the process, which would benefit the democratic consolidation in the long run. They agree to pursue democratization without violence, to settle their differences at the table rather than on the battlefield, and reach mutually acceptable agreements/compromises on democratic institutions. According to Mainwaring (1993), these classifications indicate differential positions of power in the negotiations and interactions between regimes and opposition, underscoring decisive differences in the extent to which authoritarian regimes influence the transition process. In other words, the mode of transition is a useful factor in predicting the future of new democracies.

The literature discusses pacted transitions, and describes the relative merits of negotiated transitions as either favorable or detrimental to democracy. Those who argue that pacted transitions offer the most viable path to the installation of democracy (Karl 1990; Karl and Schmitter 1991; O'Donnell and Schmitter 1986) are possibly examining pacts where the opposition holds a power advantage over incumbents, while those who argue that pacts depress competition (Karl 1987; Przeworski 1991; Hagopian 1996; Gill 2000) are examining incumbent-led transitions. In order to obtain a more refined understanding of the consequences of transitions, it is important to be aware of the ways in which the incentives and motivations of the actors transitioning the state shape outcomes.

To accomplish this, we focus on strategic choices among bargaining elites and the divergent institutional outcomes that result. We generalize the definition of pacts which serves as our point of departure from the existing literature, referring to them as "*a negotiating unit comprised of incumbent and opposition groups, attempting to bargain the transition away from authoritarian rule to democracy.*" Under this definition, pacts constitute a process that encompasses all parties that participate in transitional negotiations, with the balance of power determined by the strength of the players. Where pacts fail to exist, then transitions will most likely be violent since there is no negotiation. We could define incumbent-led pacts as those from "above" and opposition-led pacts as those from "below." Obviously, pacts can and do include exclusionary mechanisms. In order to be a party to a pact, one must have enough power to pose some type of threat to the incumbent government. In general, an incumbent-led pact will contain more exclusionary features than a pact comprised of multiple opposition groups who hold a power advantage over incumbents.

In smooth transitions, whether incumbent elites take the lead in reform or incumbent elites and opposition groups negotiate a transition, they reflect contending forces agreeing to forgo their capacity to harm each other and guarantee not to threaten each others' vital interests (Karl and Schmitter 1991; 281). According to Huntington (1991) "Negotiations and compromise among political elites were at the heart of the democratization processes. The leaders of the key political forces and social groups in society bargained with each other, explicitly or implicitly, and worked out acceptable if not satisfying arrangements for the transition to democracy" (165). The key to pacts is that they limit uncertainty associated with the transition, and provide some level of guarantees to those who potentially have a lot to either gain or lose in the transition. Viewing smooth transitions as a series of accords–agreements between the military and civilians over the establishment of civilian rule, the timing of elections, agreements between political parties to fairly compete in those elections, and social contracts between state, business, labor,[2] property rights and the distribution of benefits, is helpful in understanding the non-violent nature of these transitions. Similarly, and in contrast to violent transitions, the existing system of government is reformed, not rebuilt.

The balance of power, favoring either the opposition or incumbents, results in divergent outcomes in the adoption of institutions; these institutions have exclusionary features when incumbents lead the process and inclusionary features when the opposition does. Easter (1997) argues that the structure of old regime elites, as they emerge from the breakdown phase, determines institutional choice in the new democracy. Thus, variation in structure is determined by the continuity in the internal integrity of the old regime elites and by the extent to which incumbent elites retain access to their power resources. As discussed earlier, it is clear that one important outcome of negotiations between the regime and the opposition is the establishment of electoral rules which influence founding elections (Sutter 2000) and the subsequent development of democracy. As noted by O'Donnell and Schmitter (1986, 6)

> ...actors struggle not just to satisfy their immediate interests and/or the interests of those whom they purport to represent, but also to define rules and procedures whose configuration will determine likely winners and losers in the future. Indeed, those emergent rules will largely define which resources can legitimately be expended in the political arena and which actors will be permitted to enter it.

They note that "...during the transition, to the extent that there are any effective rules and procedures, these tend to be in the hands of authoritarian rulers" (6). I argue that an incumbent relative power advantage influences the discretionary power these rulers retain over the process of liberalization.

Under incumbent led transitions (conversion), those in power are stronger than opposition forces, and have the capacity to lead and craft the democratic reforms, and thus are expected to design reform and electoral rules that favor their party and continued rule, thus largely excluding the opposition in most cases. However, sometimes, conversion can be inclusive, with limited and controlled inclusion of opposition forces into the political process. Under conversion, consolidated old regime elites come through the breakdown phase structurally intact (Easter 1997) and do not experience severe cleavages or internal fragmentation. In these cases, opposition forces are too weak to force incumbents to alter the means of acquiring power. As a result, old regime elites retain their monopoly of power resources in the transition phase and seek the electoral reforms that they believe will benefit them the most. Karl (1990) states "Here traditional rulers remain in control, even if pressured from below, and successfully use strategies of either compromise or force – or some mix of the two – to retain at least part of their power" (17). Further, as initial elections proceed, incumbents who perform well have the incentive to continue towards a competition restricting electoral system, and this has the potential to stop and then reverse the transition. In Eastern Europe, Geddes (1996) observes that "Communist parties preferred strong presidencies, which they expected to win or appoint, and majoritarian electoral systems" (21). Even where the communists were unsure of their electoral support, they preferred the presidency, either popularly elected or appointed by parliament (Geddes 1996). Their goal was singular – to remain in power. Fearing that greater democracy will take away their privileges, incumbent elites oppose increasing democratic quality, placing them at odds with elites that prefer complete democratization (Rudra 2005, 708).

The importance of the electoral system in shaping political parties largely determines the effectiveness of the system and the performance of the government (Nohlen 1996, 45). Our argument implies that under regime conversion competition is depressed, either through specific electoral rules[3] or through the creation of rigidity in the political process that makes democratic deepening difficult. Similarly, the suppression of competition and exclusion of certain political groups is detrimental to the survival of democracy. To the extent that opposition groups are not offered a place at the table, dissatisfaction grows and the consequences potentially grave. Where opposition parties have either been banned or suppressed for many years, the continuation of a political system by incumbent elites may seem like little more than an extension of the system they sought to overthrow. As Sørensen (1993) states about elite led transitions "[they] may lead to a restricted democracy that is less capable than a nonrestricted democracy of making reform policies that go against vested elite interests" (45). If opposition groups fail to affect change under the reformed system, they may sense that a complete removal of the regime is their only option. The consequences are less democracy and a higher reversion to authoritarian rule.

Alternatively, under cooperative transitions, opposition forces are concerned with transitioning the state; their common interests are democracy and stability. Opposition forces mobilize mass support to dislodge incumbent elites from their positions of power. Old regime elites are forced to negotiate a transition to democracy (cooperate) and compete for power in the same manner as new political actors. In addition, cooperative transitions often comprise numerous competing groups who seek a role in the new democracy, along with incumbent elites, and this results in a level playing field whether through the adoption of electoral rules that maximize the ability of parties to obtain seats in the legislature or through other power-sharing arrangements. Finally, the elite in power feel themselves secured or at least not threatened by the transition, capable of playing a positive role in the transition process, and thus is more willing to cooperate and negotiate with the opposition in the transition process. As a consequence, regime-opposition cooperation is the most inclusive transition type and therefore most likely to lead to the highest posttransitional levels of democracy and survive the longest.

Suppressing competition

Competition is a core tenet of democracy. Without it, democracy does not exist. Where competition is suppressed, democracy wanes and where it is crushed, democracy dies. We argue that incumbent led transitions are detrimental for democracy because they stifle competition. Some early democratic theorists argued that restricting political competition in new democracies is necessary for their stability (see, for example, Dahl 1971). The limitations on political competition takes a variety of forms, such as restricting the policy space, banning parties, curtailing suffrage, or excluding particular groups through electoral engineering (Wright 2006). Dahl (1971) argues that democracy is most likely to endure when meaningful political contestation precedes the extension of political participation. To Dahl, when the rules and norms of competitive elections are first developed amongst a small group of elites, this is conducive to a durable democracy. As additional social groups enter the political arena, they are socialized into the rules of the democratic game. Designing a system of mutual security within a small and relatively homogeneous group of elites is much easier, and hence, more stable than designing political institutions that aggregate and balance the interests of large and diverse groups, particularly given the condition of universal suffrage.

More recently, scholars claim that unrestricted competition is destined to cause new democracies to fail because the institutions are unable to satisfy the competing economic demands of all organized sectors of society. Haggard and Kaufman (1995) posit that new democratic governments face exceptionally strong distributive pressures, both from groups reentering the political arena after long periods of repression and from established interests demanding reassurance. Thus, overwhelming the new system with demands is destined to doom it.

However, there are strong reasons to believe that unrestricted political competition makes new democracies more stable. For example, democracies that include organized groups that threaten violence if electorally excluded may be more stable. If these groups are included, they are less likely to disrupt the democratic process later on. Once relevant players start competing in the democratic game, even the losers may quickly develop a strong interest in preserving a regime that allows them the opportunity to win power in the future (Przeworski 1991). Similarly, institutional designers, under the threat of violence from excluded segments of the population, might choose higher levels of initial political competition even if they feel it is detrimental to long term democratic success.

If unfettered political competition in a new democracy reduces the incentives for potential saboteurs to subvert the regime in the future, then the converse suggests that in polities with restrictions on who can enter the new democracy, we should see evidence of conflict and the disruption of democracy. This is a compelling reason why converted transitions that formulate exclusionary policies are less durable than cooperative transitions. Civil strife occurs because those originally excluded seek power, and to obtain this power they must disrupt the democratic regime. Scholars also note that higher levels of political competition may make democracy more stable by reducing corruption (Diamond and Plattner 1993) or constraining the military (Hunter 1997). Last, there may be normative value to highly competitive democracies that endow them with legitimacy that is difficult to subvert, even in the face of economic crisis.

Wright (2006) uses data from 92 new democracies since 1946 and finds that a higher level of initial political competition in a new democracy makes for a more durable democracy. Wright's findings also suggest that new democracies with low levels of initial political competition are more likely to meet with civil conflict. Wright's findings are in direct contradiction to Dahl's argument concerning the pace of liberalizing political competition in the first years of a new democracy.[4]

The suppression of competition may be a function of whether or not the transitional government is considered interim. Violent transitions tend to be associated with interim governments, while negotiated transitions are not. According to Linz and Stepan (1996), "Interim governments are highly fluid situations and can lead to diametrically opposite outcomes depending on which groups are most powerful, and especially on whether elections or sweeping decree reforms are considered to be the first priority" (71). When interim governments quickly move towards open, free and fair elections, this can be a "very rapid and efficacious route toward a democratic transition" (71); in contrast, an interim government can manipulate power to its advantage and postpone elections until conditions are favorable for its continued rule. This is another persuasive reason that violent transitions are less likely to result in higher levels of democracy and greater longevity. The interim government may have been appointed by a foreign state and have no legitimacy, yet try to retain power and manipulate events to remain in power. Transition by pact, in contrast, results from negotiation between competing parties who have greater incentives to abide by the terms they negotiated, whether this is interim governments processing the transition of the state or more permanent governments resulting from free elections. We believe this is particularly true in cooperative transitions in which competing groups come together and negotiate institutional rules to provide a greater guarantee that elections are carried out in a timely manner, and that the electoral rules reflect greater inclusiveness.

The progression of the transitional process towards elections for representative government has a profound effect. According to O'Donnell and Schmitter (1986, 57),

> ... if it becomes credible that voters will be reasonably free in their choice – that is, existing and future parties will be free to compete by putting forth alternative candidates and that incumbents will not be free to count votes or eliminate candidacies as they see fit – then relations between contending factions and forces, inside and outside the regime, begin changing rapidly.

The occurrence of national elections brings parties together and in a position of prominence.

> If there is ever a "heroic" moment for political parties, it comes in their activity leading up to, during, and immediately following the "founding election," when, for the first time after an authoritarian regime, elected positions of national significance are disputed under reasonably competitive conditions.
>
> (O'Donnell and Schmitter 1986, 57)

Prior regime type

A significant challenge to the independent effects of transition type (Figure 3.2) on democratic success is that prior regime type determines transition type (Geddes 1999), or that prior regime type dictates the transition path available to

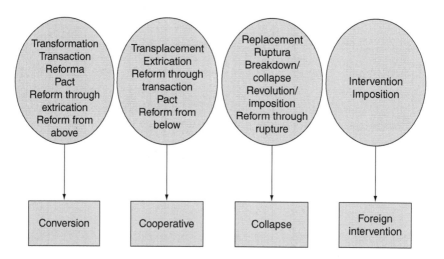

Figure 3.2 Modes of transition, a unified approach.

democratizing states (Linz and Stepan 1996). From this viewpoint, it is prior regime type that matters; the transition type is less important because the transition paths available to the autocratic regime are determined by the nature of the regime itself. According to Linz and Stepan (1996), "…the characteristics of the previous nondemocratic regime have profound implications for the transition paths available and the tasks different countries face when they begin their struggles to develop consolidated democracies" (55). Linz and Stepan (1996) theorize that regime type affects the probability and nature of regime change. Transitions from a given type of regime may have similar dynamics and explanations, but differ from transitions from other regime types (55–64). Considering the longevity and brutality of such repressive regimes, some transitioning states face a more difficult path to democracy than others. The eradication of political institutions, complete absence of opposition parties and a repressed civil society pose challenges that transitioning states from softer authoritarian regimes are spared. For example, certain authoritarian regimes in their later stages may contain a vibrant civil society and robust economic growth, thus making the path to democracy easier than a post-totalitarian communist state whose transition to democracy requires complete economic and political reform. To Linz and Stepan (1996), "…because post-totalitarian regimes have a prior totalitarian period, there will be *legacies* to overcome that are simply not found in an authoritarian regime that has never been totalitarian" (55–56). These arguments imply that Russia and Romania should have had a more difficult path to democracy than Taiwan and South Korea.

Similarly, Geddes (1999) argues that different types of authoritarian governments have varying effects on the incentives facing regime supporters when the status quo is challenged. She classifies authoritarian regimes as *military, single party* and *personalistic* and argues the type of regime that existed prior to the transition, defined according to the categories noted above, defines the domain of cases from which the causal story of transition emerges (i.e., determines the independent variables to regime transition). According to Geddes (1999), "…military regimes tend to split when challenged, personalist regimes … circle the wagons, and single-party regimes co-opt their challengers" (1). Geddes argument suggests military regimes, on average, survive less long than other types. They are more likely to negotiate their extrications and to be followed by competitive political systems. Geddes notes that they are less likely to end in coups, popular uprising, armed insurgency, revolution, invasion, or assassination. Personalist regimes, in contrast, are more likely than other types to end in violence and upheaval and their leaders rarely relinquish power voluntarily. Their departures are also more likely to be precipitated by the death of the dictator or through foreign pressure, and they are more likely to be followed by some new form of authoritarianism. Single-party regimes last the longest, but when uncontrollable popular opposition signals that the end is near, like the military, they negotiate the transition.

There is an appealing logic to the prior regime type argument but the evidence will show that its effect is not as important as is theorized. Moving a totalitarian regime to democracy seems virtually impossible through pacted negotiations but is more likely to require a violent overthrow of the government. For example, to establish democracy in North Korea under the current regime seems impossible unless removal occurs through a dominant external force, yet, many predicted the same of the Soviet Union in the late 1980s, and the U.S.S.R. initiated an incumbent-led transition. We demonstrate that the rules that emerge from the transition are a better explanation for the success or failure of democracy than the characteristics of the prior regime. That is, transition type is the determining factor of democratic success. Totalitarian regimes require economic and political reform whereas soft-authoritarian regimes only require political transition. Yet, within this realm, competition must emerge and if it is balanced and inclusive, this is a more plausible explanation for democratic success than the characteristics of the prior regime.

By creating a comprehensive dataset of democratic transitions since 1900, we test the effects of prior regime type against mode of transition. An important step in our analysis is to test prior regime type as the independent variable and transition type as the dependent variable to ascertain any independent effects of prior regime on transition type (Figure 3.3). The results will show that the prior regime type argument is not entirely accurate and that transition type provides a more satisfactory explanation of the success and/or failure of democracy. While this contradicts some of the established literature, it pushes us towards understanding the nuances of successful democratic transitions.

Hypotheses

Our theory suggests that cooperative transitions are more beneficial than other transition types. We argue that cooperative transitions result in the highest levels of democracy in the immediate posttransitional environment and are associated with the longest survival rates as they are the most inclusive. We offer two hypotheses on the causal impact of transition type on democracy:

H_1 (*The Cooperative Quality Hypothesis*): *Cooperative transitions will result in higher average levels of democracy in the posttransitional phase compared to other transitional modes.*

H_2 (*The Cooperative Duration Hypothesis*): *Cooperative transitions will have the greatest survival rate compared to other transitional modes.*

The first hypothesis suggests that cooperative transitions have a positive impact on democratic quality ratings in the posttransitional environment; the second sets forth

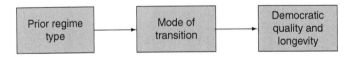

Figure 3.3 Mode of transition as intervening variable.

the proposition that cooperative transitions result in a more durable democracy. As a result, cooperative transitions reflect an *ideal* trajectory of governance in democratic growth. In this prototype model, three stages of development are associated with the process of state change: (1) the transition itself, reflected by lower levels of democracy; (2) transitional growth, reflected by increasing levels of democracy as the state builds stronger government institutions, and as the rule of law and civil society emerge; and (3) democratic consolidation, typified as a "safe zone" for democracy with minimal or no likelihood of reversion to authoritarian rule. Similar to Kadera's (2001) use of the population model in which a state's power naturally expands over time until it reaches the maximum level of resources to sustain its population, the application of the model to democratic government reflects increasing levels of democracy to the point of consolidation, when democratic levels continue to rise, but at a much slower pace (see Figure 3.4).

Geddes (1999) argues that prior regime type determines transition type. The implication of her argument is that prior regime type will subvert the independent effects of transition type on democracy. Therefore we must test the following hypotheses which are derived from Geddes' argument. They allow us to determine if transition type is a more plausible explanation of successful democracy than mode of transition:

H₃ (*Peaceful Military Transition*): *Military regimes are more likely to result in either a conversion or cooperative transition.*

H₄ (*Violent Personalistic Transition*): *Personalistic regimes are more likely to transition through a collapse or foreign intervention.*

H₅ (*Peaceful Single Party Regime Transition*): *Single party regimes are more likely to result in either a cooperative or conversion transition.*

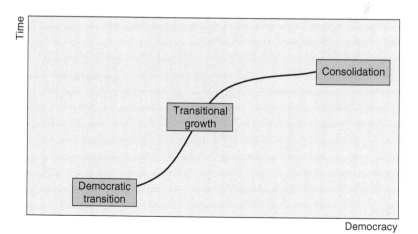

Figure 3.4 Prototype democratic growth after transition.

Based on our expected findings in relation to cooperative transitions, we will have to analyze the results for H_3–H_5. If, for example, we find that H_3 is accepted (that military regimes transition through negotiation), an important next step is to determine the breakdown of transition type (i.e., whether the military regime is transitioning through conversion or cooperation) and test the impact this has on democratic quality and duration. To the extent that any of Geddes' arguments hold, then transition type constitutes another explanation of successful democratization, albeit an alternative one. If prior regime type does not determine transition type, then mode of transition exerts a greater independent effect on democracy than the prior regime argument suggests.

In this chapter, we have advanced a theory to explain the success rate of democratic transitions and argued that cooperative transitions result in the highest levels of democracy in the posttransitional phase, in addition to surviving the longest. The reason for this is that when incumbents and opposition groups work together to make the democratic transition, they work within an inclusive environment that affects the transitional process in many ways, including constitutional design and the adoption of electoral rules. The inclusivity of this process maximizes competition and therefore satisfaction among competing groups. Further, the populace is inclined to believe that their vote counts and that the new democratic system functions in a capacity that is more than an extension of its authoritarian predecessor. When satisfaction among competing groups is high and the losses in one election have the potential to be overcome with gains in the next, and elites believe this and therefore do not attempt to subvert the system, democracy works as it should. Our next step is to test quantitatively the hypotheses deduced from our theory of explaining the success rate of democratic transitions.

Notes

1 Remarks made by Freedom House Chairman Peter Ackerman in the conference on Democracy and Security, June 5–6, 2007, Prague, Czech Republic.
2 For an analysis on the role of labor as a fundamental causal force in the move towards democracy, see: Ruth Collier. 1999. *Paths toward Democracy: The Working Class and Elites in Western Europe and South America.* New York: Cambridge University Press.
3 With regard to electoral rules adopted we make no claims as to whether presidentialism or parliamentarism is more conducive to successful democracy.
4 Wright (2006) explains political competition as "…whether or not institutional restrictions are placed on groups that might otherwise participate in the democratic game" (228). Wright employs the Polity IV measure of political competition (PARCOM), a five-point ordinal index scale (5 is the highest) that measures the extent to which alternative preferences for policy and leadership can be pursued in the political arena. According to Wright, "While this measure of political competition may be a rather blunt measure, it does capture meaningful variation in how much latitude different groups in society have to pursue political power" (228).

References

Ackerman, Peter. 2007. *How Freedom Is Won.* Conference on Democracy and Security sponsored through Freedom House. Czernin Palace, Czech Republic, June 5–6.

Andrews, Josephine T. and Robert W. Jackman. 2005. "Strategic Fools: Electoral Rule Choice under Extreme Uncertainty." *Electoral Studies* 24: 65–84.

Benoit, Kenneth and John W. Schiemann. 2001. "Institutional Choice in New Democracies: Bargaining over Hungary's 1989 Electoral Law." *Journal of Theoretical Politics* 13(2): 159–188.

Blechman, Barry M. and Stephen S. Kaplan. 1978. *Force without War*. Washington DC: Brookings Institute Press.

Bueno de Mesquita, Bruce, Alastair Smith, Randolph M. Siverson and James D. Morrow. 2003. *The Logic of Political Survival*. Cambridge: The MIT Press.

Colomer, Josep M. 2000. *Strategic Transitions: Game Theory and Democratization*. Baltimore: The Johns Hopkins University Press.

Dahl, Robert A. 1971. *Polyarchy: Participation and Opposition*. New Haven: Yale University Press.

Diamond, Larry and Marc Plattner. 1993. *Global Resurgence of Democracy*. Baltimore: Johns Hopkins University Press.

Duverger, Maurice. 1954. *Political Parties*. New York: Wiley.

Easter, Gerald M. 1997. "Preference for Presidentialism: Postcommunist Regime Change in Russia and the NIS." *World Politics* 49(2): 194–211.

Geddes, Barbara. 1996. "Initiation of New Democratic Institutions in Eastern Europe and Latin America." In *Institutional Design in New Democracies: Eastern Europe and Latin America*, ed. Arend Lijphart and Carlos H. Waisman. Boulder, Colorado: Westview Press.

Geddes, Barbara. 1999. "Authoritarian Breakdown: Empirical Test of a Game Theoretic Approach." *Paper prepared for the annual meeting of the American Political Science Association*, Atlanta, Georgia.

Gill, Graeme. 2000. *The Dynamics of Democratization: Elites, Civil Society and the Transition Process*. New York: St. Martin's Press.

Haggard, Stephan and Robert R. Kaufman. 1995. *The Political Economy of Democratic Transitions*. New Jersey: Princeton University Press.

Hagopian, Frances. 1996. *Traditional Politics and Regime Change in Brazil*. New York: Cambridge University Press.

Huntington, Samuel P. 1991. *The Third Wave: Democratization in the Late Twentieth Century*. Norman: University of Oklahoma Press.

Hunter, Wendy. 1997. *Eroding Military Influence in Brazil: Politicians against Soldiers*. Chapel Hill, NC: University of North Carolina Press.

Kadera, Kelly M. 2001. *The Power-Conflict Story: A Dynamic Model of Interstate Rivalry*. Ann Arbor: The University of Michigan Press.

Karl, Terry Lynn. 1987. "Petroleum and Political Pacts." *Latin American Research Review* 22: 63–94.

Karl, Terry Lynn. 1990. "Dilemmas of Democratization in Latin America." *Comparative Politics* 23(1): 1–21.

Karl, Terry Lynn and Philippe C. Schmitter. 1991. "Modes of transition in Latin America, Southern and Eastern Europe." *International Social Science Journal* 128: 269–284.

Lijphart, Arend. 1992. "Democratization and Constitutional Choices in Czecho-Slovakia, Hungary and Poland, 1989–91." *Journal of Theoretical Politics* 4: 207–223.

Linz, Juan and Alfred Stepan. 1996. *Problems of Democratic Transition and Consolidation: Southern Europe, South America and Post-Communist Europe*. Baltimore: The Johns Hopkins University Press.

Mainwaring, Scott. 1993. "Presidentialism, Multipartism, and Democracy: The Difficult Combination." *Comparative Political Studies* 26: 198–228.

Nohlen, Dieter. 1996. *Elections and Electoral Systems.* New Delhi: Macmillan.

O'Donnell, Guillermo and Philippe Schmitter. 1986. *Transitions from Authoritarian Rule: Tentative Conclusions about Uncertain Democracies.* Baltimore: The Johns Hopkins University Press.

Przeworski, Adam. 1991. *Democracy and the Market.* New York: Cambridge University Press.

Rosenau, J. 1969. "Intervention as a Scientific Concept." *Journal of Conflict Resolution* 12(2): 149–171.

Rudra, Nita. 2005. "Globalization and the Strengthening of Democracy in the Developing World." *American Journal of Political Science* 49(4): 704–730.

Saxer, Carl J. 2003. "Democratic Transition and Institutional Crafting: The South Korean Case." *Democratization* 10(2): 45–64.

Sørensen, Georg. 1993. *Democracy and Democratization.* Boulder: Westview Press.

Sutter, Daniel. 2000. "The Transitions from Authoritarian Rule: A Game Theoretic Approach." *Journal of Theoretical Politics* 12(1): 67–89.

Ward, Michael D. and Kristian S. Gleditsch. 1998. "Democratizing for Peace." *American Political Science Review* 92(1): 52–62.

Wright, Joseph. 2006. "Political Competition and Democratic Stability in New Democracies." *British Journal of Political Science* 38: 221–245.

4 Research design and empirics

The focus of the theory, developed in the preceding chapters as well as the empirical results discussed in this chapter, comprise countries transitioning towards democracy. Therefore, the unit of analysis is the democratizing nation-state. Every nation since 1900 undergoing a democratic transition is included, for a total of 130 cases. In identifying transitions from authoritarianism to democratic rule, we draw on a variety of sources including Huntington's *The Third Wave* (1991), seminal works by Linz (1978) and Share and Mainwaring (1986), the updated Political Regime Change dataset (1996), Polity IV Country Reports (2006) and extensive qualitative historical case study analyses from journal articles and other scholarly writings.

Huntington's work concentrates on regime transitions since 1973 while the Political Regime Change dataset, created by Gasiorowski (1996) and updated by Reich (2002), contains a regime classification for over 150 countries from the founding of the state through December 1998, with regimes identified as democratic, semi-democratic or authoritarian. The Polity IV Country Reports provide an historical overview of major events (e.g., elections, coups and key events between incumbents and opposition groups that led to regime change) for all nations within the Polity dataset, which essentially includes any country with a population greater than 500,000. Each dataset has its limitations. Since Huntington's work is restricted to transitions since 1973 (the so-called *Third Wave* transitions), it provides no insight into democratizing countries for the majority of the twentieth century. On the other hand, the works by Linz (1978) and Share and Mainwaring (1986) are regionally focused. The Political Regime Change Dataset is broader in scope and cover countries in Latin America, the Middle East, Africa and Asia; however, it only examines post-World War II changes or those occurring after 1944.

For purposes of this study, we utilize these widely accepted works of transitions as a baseline comparison of regime change to both determine and adopt consistency in coding of countries. Under the best scenario, the various sources will agree on how regime change occurs in any particular country; however, due to the regional focus of many studies, it is mostly not possible to compare the coding of cases across studies. Further, we do not strictly rely on the coding of others but rather, we evaluate various qualitative historical sources to make a definitive determination of when and how a transition occurred. As discussed in Chapter 2, our primary coding rule for transitional modes is to determine the *trigger event* by country in order to achieve a consistent methodology of classifications. Unlike prior studies, which often take an ad hoc approach to classifying regime change, using a trigger event provides a consistent and reasonable method to determine how democratic transitions started (i.e., what key event occurred to start the change from authoritarianism to democracy?). Our goal was to create an expanded dataset that covers all countries in the world transitioning since 1900[1] in an effort to draw generalizations across regions and time (Appendix A), an important contribution of this study. In all, we study regime change in 130 countries and measure democracy scores over approximately 1,300 country years. Similar to any study on transitioning states, our coding is not dogmatic as we are aware of complicated issues surrounding complex historical events that define the democratic transition. However, we are confident that the results are not an artifact of coding decisions and we perform various robustness checks to determine the validity of the results (see Appendix B).

Independent variables

They key independent variables are the four modes of transition to democracy – *conversion* (where the elites in power take the lead in transitioning the state), *cooperative* (where opposition groups with a power advantage over incumbents take the lead in transitioning the state), *collapse* (where opposition groups violently overthrow the incumbent regime) and *foreign intervention* (where a dominant external power removes an authoritarian regime for the purposes of establishing a democratic government). For a discussion of the four transition types, refer to Chapter 2. Here, we discuss the decision rules for coding transitioning states.

Regime collapse and foreign intervention are relatively straightforward transition types and therefore the easiest to code, and the trigger events in both countries clearly indicate such. For example, the mode of transition in Afghanistan and Iraq in 2001 and 2003 respectively were clearly the result of military intervention by United States and Coalition forces. Additionally, Panama (1989–90) and Haiti (1984) transitioned via foreign intervention. In these countries, the United States military forcefully removed the incumbent regime and facilitated its replacement with a democratic one. Here, the causal and necessary mechanism to facilitate democracy was foreign military intervention. Regime collapse is also relatively straightforward to identify compared to negotiated transitions: Thailand (1992), Romania (1989) and the Philippines (1986). Alternatively, while negotiated transitions are not necessarily difficult to determine, it is the balance of power in the transition that poses the greatest problem (i.e., determining whether incumbents or opposition groups took the lead in transitioning the state). Only through detailed historical qualitative analysis can this be resolved and it requires a nuanced evaluation of the trigger event to ascertain the course of action that led to democracy.

Among the four classifications lie a large number of "mixed" transitions, encompassing features of more than one mode of transition. Mixed transitions are the most difficult to classify, such as Chile in the 1980s. For example, Munck and Leff (1997) categorize Chile as *reform from below*, Huntington (1991) as *transformation*, and Karl and Schmitter (1991) place it somewhere between *imposition* and *pact*.[2] Other cases present similar difficulties, such as Argentina, Greece, Peru and Zambia. Nonetheless, determining the trigger event will help identify the starting point of the democratization process.

To continue with the example of Chile, we determined the trigger event as taking place in October of 1988, when General Pinochet submitted himself to a "yes" or "no" vote on his continued rule. Pinochet was attempting to demonstrate his control over the early process of liberalization in addition to prior commitments he had made to restore democracy. Encouraged by strong economic growth, Pinochet viewed the upcoming elections as an opportunity to restore legitimacy to his rule. Nonetheless, he overestimated voter sentiment and lost the election 55 percent to 43 percent. In classifying Chile's transition, the following is noted: prior to the plebiscite, Pinochet's government was stronger than the opposition group and was therefore the impetus for change. In other words, Pinochet, holding the upper hand, could have simply refused to hold the election. After losing the election, Pinochet's government led the reform process, albeit under growing pressure, as was evident in Pinochet's transfer of power to Patricio Aylwin, the new democratically elected president, in 1990. The loss paved the way for increased influence of the opposition in the transition; however, Pinochet's power continued as he retained the post of commander-in-chief of the army until 1998, when he assumed a seat in the Chilean Senate. Despite Pinochet's defeat, Sørensen (1993) notes "Pinochet [is] able to restrict the new democracy in vital areas and preserve a high degree of influence for nondemocratic organs" (48). In Chile, democratization commenced through ruling elite action, although the outcome was unintended. Thus, Chile is a case of transition by *conversion*.

Dependent variable

The dependent variable in this study is the level of democracy (i.e., quality) within each democratizing country over a ten-year interval. To analyze a country's level of democracy, we use the Polity IV (2004) index. Democracy indices identify the degree to which a country is either democratic or authoritarian and therefore suitable to a study concerned with measuring both the quality of democracy and its longevity – Polity IV allows us to do both. In addition to Polity IV (2004), Freedom House (1998) is the most common measures of democracy and is widely used in scholarly studies; however, Freedom House does not start measuring democracy until 1973 and our study covers all democratizing countries since 1900 (or the date they came into existence) to 1998.[3] Robert Dahl notes "Although at this point a complete, reliable, and current account of all democratic countries in the world appears to be unavailable, the two datasets

Polity (IV) and Freedom House allow fairly good estimates of democratization" (1998, 199). Thus, while we can debate the individual merits of any particular democracy rating, using Polity IV provides for consistency as well as utility as a widely accepted and used coding schematic in scholarly studies.

For the dependent variable, we measure the level of democracy for years 1–10 after the coded date of the mode of transition, or when Polity IV scores emerge from a transitional coding scheme to actual democracy ratings.[4] Polity IV scores capture the level of democracy as calculated from an index based on each country's annual rating for political competition and executive restraints. It ranges from −10 (least democratic political institutions) to 10 (most democratic political institutions). Polity IV is a weighted indicator comprising three components: the presence of democratic institutions and procedures, institutional checks on the exercise of power, and individual freedom and right to political participation, which are conceptually consistent with the key elements of democracy and the basic framework of assessing the quality of democracy developed by one of the best-known experts in the field of democracy theory and practice (Beetham 2002).

Polity IV scores are used extensively in comparative politics and international relations. More importantly, all of the indicators used to construct the index are accessible and well documented. The Polity IV dataset characterizes political systems using a set of various indicators (Gurr 1974; Marshall, Jaggers and Gurr 2007) and contains information for all countries with a population over 500,000 for the period 1800 to 2000. These indicators are grouped to form variables describing systems along three authority dimensions. The first dimension is the regulation of *Executive Recruitment* based on three indicators: regulation of chief executive recruitment, competitiveness of executive recruitment and openness of executive recruitment. The second dimension is *Constraints on the Executive* and based on a single indicator decision constraints on the chief executive." The third dimension concerns *Political Participation*.

Thus, Polity IV scores are designed to provide a scaled description of "polities," based on "authority patterns." The five expert-coded categorical indicators are all capable of being ordered: (1) competitiveness of executive recruitment, (2) openness of executive recruitment, (3) executive constraints/decision rules, (4) regulation of participation, and (5) competitiveness of participation. Further, Polity IV correlates at 0.85 with other accepted measures of democracy such as Freedom House. Polity data are also used to measure democracy as both dependent and independent variables in many respected and widely cited studies (e.g., Hartman and Hsiao 1988; Nagle 1985; Scoble and Wiseberg 1981; Ward and Gleditsch 1998; Gates *et al.* 2006). Polity scores measured over time are consistent with the concept of democratic sustainability and consolidation. Higher levels of democracy reflect greater relative levels of democratic quality. Measuring Polity scores over time captures reversion,[5] stagnation and progression associated with the mode of transition. For example, a country with a Polity score of 10, measured in year 10, is a strong indicator that reversion to authoritarianism is highly unlikely and that democracy is institutionalized. For the 130 cases in this study, we measure Polity scores ten years after the transition. We use ten years as a cut-off point because the data indicates that once a state has remained democratic for ten years, the possibility of a reversion to dictatorship is minimal.[6] In the dataset, the only state to survive as a democracy for ten years and then revert to dictatorship is Greece. In 1926 Greece became democratic and then reverted to dictatorship in 1936. Alternatively, a state with Polity scores of 6, 5, 3, –2 and –2 in years 1, 3, 5, 7 and 10 after the transition captures a democratic reversal. In this example, our sample country is moderately democratic in years 1, 3 and 5 and then reverts by years 7 and 10. However, inferences about the quality of democracy reflect the fact that democracy is a latent variable, measured indirectly with a limited number of imperfect indicators and subject to measurement error.

For the dependent variable, we do not start measuring Polity IV scores when the actual process of liberalization starts; it is simply not possible, nor necessary, to do this since Polity IV reflects a "transitional process" score for many nations rather than a democratic rating as the process of state change starts. Polity scores for some countries (especially those gradually liberalizing) show a softening of the authoritarian regime but cannot be considered democratic until the first national election. For example, an incumbent-elite-led process may begin years before the first democratic election, such as in Taiwan when then-President Chiang Ching-kuo liberalized the system and allowed opposition parties to exist starting in 1986. Alternatively, where change is rapid, the overthrow of the government is often followed by elections in a matter of months (East Germany went from a Polity score of –9 in 1988 to a 10 in 1991). The difficulty in measurement is apparent in these cases; elite-guided transformation processes often reflect a steady softening of the authoritarian regime, leading to gradual democracy ratings, while in a collapse, Polity scores reflect a democratic rating within a couple of years.

To measure the dependent variable with Polity IV scores, we start from the first democratic national election. This is also an artifact of the data source. In Taiwan, for example, we qualitatively evaluated the mode of transition and determined the trigger event as Chiang's liberalization policies beginning in 1986. Since Chiang was the incumbent ruler and led the reform process with the ruling party, the mode of transition was incumbent led; at the time, there was little input from the opposition. As a result, Taiwan transitioned by conversion. The reform process accelerated over the next five years and the first national election was held in December of 1991. We then reviewed the Polity scores for Taiwan during this period. On the eve of reform, in 1986, Taiwan had a Polity IV score of –7. From 1987 to 991, the Polity score improved dramatically to a –1 which reflected a softening of the authoritarian regime, a direct result of Chiang's liberalization policies. Finally, in 1992, after the first national election, the Polity score increased to 7, clearly indicating a democratic polity. We begin measuring the dependent variable in 1992 which is consistent with our coding rule of starting from the first democratic national election. To clarify, the mode of transition (the independent variable) is determined by the trigger event (a singular or series of events that starts a country's movement towards democracy), while the first national election is used as the measurement starting point of the dependent variable. Clearly there is a lag between the two; however it is a reasonable way to proceed because it provides consistency in coding of both the independent and dependent variables.

Iraq highlights an important point and provides an example of an exception to the coding procedure we use. Iraq is currently occupied by U.S. and Coalition forces and the Polity rating reflects a –66 for "interruption" due to this occupation. Even though Iraq had a democratic national election in 2005, we cannot start coding Iraq until the interruption coding is replaced with actual Polity scores that meet our minimal definition of democracy. Similarly, many of the European post-World War II cases (i.e., those countries occupied by Nazi Germany) are coded as –66 during the war years and then emerge with democratic Polity scores starting in 1944–45. In the case of Iraq, the country must stand on its own, whether that is through a significantly scaled-down foreign occupation or complete liberation and autonomy from a foreign power, before Polity IV scores will reflect ratings other than "interruption."

Polity IV scores reflect democratic ratings or substantial regime change following the emergence of the nation-state from an interruption phase (civil war, foreign occupation) or the first democratic national election (autonomous from foreign occupation). For each democratic Polity score, a trigger event started the transition to democracy that ultimately led to a competitive national election. Above all, a regime cannot be considered democratic until it has held a free election and using the first democratic election provides a consistent starting point from which to measure cases (therefore, the cases in this study comprise transitions that succeed by a minimalistic measure of democracy initially, and excludes those transitions that never reach this threshold). Our cut-off point for a democracy is a Polity IV score of 5. While this is the lower end of what constitutes democracy, its sine qua non is competitive elections. Excluding cases that never reach a democratic threshold is not problematic as we are only concerned with understanding how the mode of transition influences the resultant democracy – both its quality and sustainability. For example, there were democratic elements within the 1979 Iranian Revolution (the trigger event being a regime collapse) that quickly lost out to authoritarian theocratic elites. Since Iran never achieved a first democratic election, it is not included in the dataset. In this regard, we weed out transitions that do not culminate in a first competitive national election, even where those transitions possessed some democratic elements.

In evaluating Polity scores, most transitions are clear and this provides strong confirmation of the qualitative findings on the independent variable. For example, it is more common to see countries make large movements from, for example, a –7 in one year to a 5 in the next, rather than an incremental movement from a 2 to a 3. This facilitates the coding of the dependent variable. Our decision rule for a transition is that the change from t to $t+1$ is 3 or more Polity points. Therefore, a change from a 2 to a 5 constitutes a democratic transition but a change from a 4 to a 5 does not (typically a change from a 4 to a 5 is not associated with any trigger event). Fortunately, the latter is so rare, if non-existent, that it does not pose a coding problem. In addition, if a country moves from a –9 in *t* and then to a 3 in *t*+1, we cannot code this as a transition even though something significant happened (since 3 does not reach the cut-off point of 5). Most likely, the nation transitioned from a brutal dictatorship to a soft authoritarian regime. For example, in 1907 Portugal had a Polity score of –9 and a score of 2 in 1908. The assassination of King Carlos I started a series of events that led to the ousting of the dictator João Franco in 1908 by the new king, Manuel II. Free elections were declared although the last King of Portugal would be ousted in a coup three years later. For purposes of examining democratic reversals and the termination of democracy, we code a democratic death as taking place when the Polity score drops below 5. That is, if a country drops from a 5 to a 4 in the course of a year, we code this as a reversion to authoritarianism and censor the case (i.e., for determining democratic duration via the proportional hazard model). We do not examine trigger events that return democratic polities to authoritarian regimes as this is not the purpose of this study – that is suited to a study that examines transitions to dictatorship and the failure of democracy.

For nations emerging after World War II, we only code those countries as having a democratic transition if they had been authoritarian prior to the War and then democratic thereafter. For example, from 1934 to 1937, Austria had a Polity IV rating of –9, indicating the country was strictly authoritarian. In 1946 the Polity IV score was 10; therefore, we code Austria as having a democratic transition (i.e., Austria was a dictatorship prior to the war but became democratic thereafter). Czechoslovakia, up to 1939, had a Polity IV rating of 7, and then a rating of –77** (transitional coding) from 1939 to 1944, and then a 10 from 1945 to 1946. We do not code Czechoslovakia as a democratic transition because it was a democracy prior to the war. It is not appropriate to code Czechoslovakia as transitioning in 1945 since the country had been democratic prior to war, was interrupted by foreign occupation and then became democratic again after it was liberated. These are not democratic transitions but rather liberations from aggressor countries that returned them to their prior democratic status.

Other independent variables (controls)

As control variables, we employ a standard set of indicators expected to have an influence on the success and duration of democracy, including prior regime type, prior democratic history, region, institutional choice, and modernization indicators of per capita GDP and annual economic growth rates.

Prior regime type

Prior regime type functions as a control variable in the main models as we are concerned with determining whether or not it influences the quality and duration

Table 4.1 Dependent and independent variable coding rules

Dependent variable	Independent variable
1. Polity IV score must reach a 5 (the minimum threshold for a democracy) for the case to be considered a democratic transition; *and*	A trigger event is determined – a formative event or series of events that starts the process of democratization
2. The transition must be signified by a change of 3 or more Polity points from t to $t+1$ (and must reach a minimum Polity IV score of 5)	The characteristics of the event and who exerts the most influence in the event determines how the case is coded
3. WWII cases – only countries that were authoritarian prior to the war and then democratic afterwards are considered democratic transitions. Democracies prior to the war and then occupied by Nazi Germany during the war and liberated thereafter are not considered democratic transitions	
4. Democratic Reversion – any country that drops below a Polity IV of 5 is considered a democratic reversal and the case is censored	

of democracy. A compelling alternative explanation is that prior regime type exerts a strong effect on transition type (more so than mode of transition) and therefore in our second model, we utilize it as the key explanatory variable with transition type as the dependent variable. Prior research shows that different types of authoritarian regimes break down in distinct ways because key cadres in those regimes have differing interests and face varying strategic environments (Geddes 1999). By implication, this dictates the transition path available to the authoritarian regime. In the extreme, it means that transition type is an intervening variable, determined by the type of prior regime, which exerts a greater impact on democracy – more so than the nature of the transition. Alternatively, transition type functions as an alternative, yet plausible, explanation in the democratization process. For example, regardless of how the path to democracy is determined, the transition is when the rules of the new democracy are formulated. Thus, transitions are complex events that are not pre-determined from the legacy of the authoritarian regime. To measure prior regime type, we rely on Geddes' (1999) study on authoritarian breakdown, in addition to examining qualitative historical records to ascertain the type of the prior authoritarian regime. In all instances, as we worked through coding the mode of transition, we gained insight into the type of prior regime. Based on the theory developed in Chapter 3, we do not expect to find prior regime type variables to reach statistical significance.

Prior democratic history

While we believe democratization can progress in states without a democratic tradition, it is necessary to control for prior democratic history due to an abundant literature asserting this claim. According to Feng and Zak (1999), on average, a country with a prior democratic experience is about five times more likely to make a full democratic transition (174). To determine if a country possessed a prior democratic history, we first reviewed Polity IV scores dating back to 1900 (i.e., locating countries with Polity ratings of at least 5 to maintain consistency with the coding rules of this study), in addition to examining various historical volumes to verify the accuracy of the Polity IV indicator.

Region

Region is an exogenous variable that potentially influences democratization via forces within the region where a country resides; these forces are sometimes referred to as diffusion processes (Wejnert 2005, 53) or snowballing effects. We control for region because countries in some geographic locations are more likely to be democratic than others (e.g., Western Europe at the end of World War II became mostly democratic as did many states in Eastern Europe after the Cold War). It is impossible to ignore that the majority of Europe is democratic, while the Middle East and Africa remains largely authoritarian. It is difficult to ascertain why transitions are more prevalent in certain regions and some competing explanations refer to common or similar culture, social structure, religion, institutions, and economic changes. In the case of Latin American transitions, Mainwaring and Pérez-Liñán (2005), state that "The strongest finding of the quantitative analysis is that a regional environment that was more favorable to democracy was a key factor" (25). Huntington (1991) suggested that democratization in one country encouraged democratization in other countries and referred to this as "demonstration" or "snowballing" effects. The rationale for contagion effects is that successful democratization elsewhere is viewed as a cure for problems in other authoritarian countries, or perhaps the country that has democratized is powerful and viewed as a political and cultural model. Understanding whether region asserts an effect on democratic success would lead us to further examine why democracy succeeds in some parts of the world but not in others. For example, Feng and Zak (1999) empirically demonstrate "The negative impact on democratic transitions of being a Muslim nation is more pronounced than of being a Pacific Asian nation" (174). However, this argument diminishes over time as today democracy exists in every region of the world although it is more prevalent in some areas than in others. Further, as discussed in Chapter 1, the time interval between the proliferation of Western democracy and the gradual spread to the rest of world is relatively small.

Institutional choice

Institutional choice has a prolific literature when discussing democratizing countries. Hermens (1941) argues that parliamentary democracies are prone to breakdown, while others claim that presidential democracies are more unstable (Linz 1978, 1994). In the "Perils of Presidentialism" Linz (1990) posits that certain features of presidential regimes – fixed terms in office and winner-takes-all elections – contribute to rigidity in the political process, inadequate representation, dual executive and legislative authority and a fragmented party system. Some empirical research supports Linz's thesis (Stepan and Skach 1993; Przeworski *et al.* 2000), some qualifies it (Mainwaring 1993, Mainwaring and Shugart 1997), and some challenges it (Gasiorowski and Power 1997). Svolik (2008) empirically finds that a presidential executive reduces the odds that a democracy consolidates (154). Alternatively, Cheibub (2007) revisits the findings between presidentialism and democratic survival and after various empirical tests concludes "what kills democracy is not presidentialism but rather the military legacy inherited from the prior regime" (140). Controlling for institutional choice therefore becomes important to determine if parliamentary, presidential or mixed systems are more likely to contribute to the success or failure of democracy. By controlling for institutional choice, we can determine if certain electoral systems are in part to blame for the breakdown of democracies or are associated with lower levels of democratic quality. Alternatively, we can determine if institutional choice has a strong effect on the probability that democracy will succeed. We have no expected finding as to which institutional choice is best for democracy. Concerning institutional choice and its impact on success in new democracies, O'Donnell and Schmitter (1986) say, "There can be no hard-and-fast answer to this question" (60). Each national case has to experiment and draw on the lessons of others in order to find the solution that works best for them.

GDP per capita and annual economic growth rates

Perhaps the most prolific and important literature concerning the survival of democracy centers on economic growth.[7] Thus, controlling for per capita GDP is important because of the controversy about whether wealth helps democracy to consolidate (Rueschemeyer 1991, Diamond 1992), or merely assists democracies in surviving after a transition (Przeworski and Limongi 1997). Regardless of the causal factors that lead to democratization, higher levels of per capita GDP, according to a widely accepted literature, should help prevent slippage back into autocracy. Przeworski (1991) states, "...the eventual survival of ... new democracies will depend to a large extent on their economic performance" (95). In a later work, Przeworski *et al.* (2000) suggest that once countries transition to democracy, those with higher levels of per capita GDP are likely to remain democratic. Epstein *et al.* (2006), who challenge Przeworski on a number of points, also agree that "...higher GDP per capita reduces the probability that countries fall out of democracy" (564). Rising living standards, growth of private ownership and of the urban middle classes and improved education arguably constitute the main forces that lead people to support democratic procedures (Evans and Whitefield 1995); this support of democratic procedures not only serves as an impetus to democracy but also facilitates its survival. Therefore, we expect the coefficient on per capita GDP to be positive and significant. In addition, we control for GDP growth rate and expect higher growth rates to be associated with higher democratic quality and greater longevity. Intuitively, a regime that provides strong growth would seem to suffer less from legitimacy problems and therefore be at a lower risk of reversion. The authoritative source of historical GDP is obtained from Angus Maddison.[8] Through use of this dataset, we have access to per capita GDP for all countries of the world from the start date of our study (1900) through 2003. We calculate the corresponding growth rates based on the dollar changes in GDP.

Empirical results and analysis

To test the main premises of the theory, we develop two core models that encompass various questions (see Figure 4.1). First, in Model I, we seek to understand the impact of the explanatory variable (mode of transition) on the dependent variables – the quality and duration of democracy. Thus, the question we test in Model I is: Do modes of transition matter? In Model II, we directly test the assertions made by Geddes (1999) that prior regime type dictates the transition path available to states. In order to do this, we formulate five separate hypotheses. The model specifications are as follows:

Model I

The hypotheses and core model specifications are represented in the following equations which are directly derived from the theory specified in Chapter 3:

H_1 (*The Cooperative Quality Hypothesis*): *Cooperative transitions will result in higher average levels of democracy in the posttransitional phase compared to other transitional modes.*[9]

$H_{1(model)}$: $PY_t = \beta_0 + \beta_1$ (Transition Type) $+ \beta_2$ (Region) $+ \beta_3$ (Institutional Choice) $+ \beta_4$ (Prior Regime Type) $+ \beta_5$ (Prior Dem History) $+ \beta_6$ (per capita GDP_t) $+ \beta_7 (GDP_{gr}) + \varepsilon$

In H_2, we measure democratic duration, or the longevity of democracy, as the dependent variable which is reflected in the proportional hazard model:

H_2 (*The Cooperative Duration Hypothesis*): *Cooperative transitions will have the greatest survival rate compared to other transitional modes.*

$H_{2(model)}$: Duration of Democracy$(t) = \lambda_0(t) \exp \{\beta_0 + \beta_1$ (Transition Type) $+ \beta_2$ (Institutional Choice) $+ \beta_3$ (Prior Regime Type) $+ \beta_4$ (Prior Democratic History) $+ \beta_5$ (per capita GDP_t) $+ \beta_6 (GDP_{gr}) + \varepsilon$

Model II

To examine Geddes' (1999) findings, we test the claims in Model II using multinomial logistic regression. Directly based on her findings, we formulate and test the following hypotheses:

H_3 (*Peaceful Military Transition*): *Military regimes are more likely to result in either a conversion or cooperative transition.*

H_4 (*Violent Personalistic Transition*): *Personalist regimes are more likely to transition through a collapse or foreign intervention.*

H_5 (*Peaceful Single Party Regime Transition*): *Single party regimes are more likely to result in either a cooperative or conversion transition.*

$H_{3-5(models)}$: Transition Type$_t = \beta_0 + \beta_1$ (Prior Regime Type) $+ \beta_2$ (Prior Democratic History) $+ \beta_3$ (Region) $+ \varepsilon$

We next determine if prior regime type influences democratic quality and duration. If Geddes arguments hold, then it becomes necessary to explore whether prior regime types that result in negotiated transitions impact democratic quality and duration. We expect that prior regime types that result in cooperative

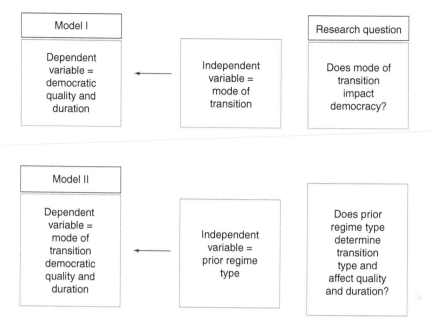

Figure 4.1 Research design.

transitions (i.e., military and single party regimes) will have the highest levels of democracy and last the longest. The following hypotheses test these claims:

> H_6 (*The Military and Single Party Quality Hypothesis*): *Military and single party regimes will have higher average levels of democracy in the posttransitional phase compared to personalistic regimes.*

> H_7 (*The Military and Single Party Duration Hypothesis*): *Military and single party regimes will have the greatest survival rates compared to personalistic regimes.*

$H_{6(model)}$: $PY_t = \beta_0 + \beta_1$ (Prior Regime Type) $+ \varepsilon$

$H_{7(model)}$: Duration of Democracy $(t) = \lambda_0(t)$ exp $\{\beta_0 + \beta_1$ (Prior Regime Type) $+ \varepsilon$

The goal of the statistical analysis is to determine the independent effects of transition type on democratic quality and longevity. The basis of our theoretical argument as expressed in H_1 and H_2 are that modes of transition are the most important predictors of a country's democratic success and/or failure. Rather than serving as an intervening variable between prior regime type and democratic outcomes as implied by Geddes (1999), we seek to show the independent effects of transition type on democracy. Therefore, first we must demonstrate that H_1 and H_2 have merit; second, we must show that prior regime type is less important in explaining both the mode of transition available to states, in addition to having a minimal effect on democratic quality and duration. The variables in the models are:

PY: Polity score measured at varying intervals
Transition type: the mode of transition from authoritarian rule (conversion (baseline), cooperative, collapse and foreign intervention)
Region: North America (baseline), Europe, North Africa and Middle East, South America, Asia and Pacific and Sub-Saharan Africa
Institutional choice: presidential (baseline), parliamentary and mixed
Prior regime type: military (baseline); single party, personalistic and prior colony
Prior democratic history: yes (baseline); no
Per capita GDP_t: per capita gross domestic product at time t
GDP_{gr}: gross domestic product growth rate at time t

Statistical methodology

To test the H_1 *(Cooperative Quality Hypothesis)*, we utilize ordinary least squares regression (OLS) and estimate robust standard errors. OLS is used rather than logit due to the large variation in the dependent variable (Polity IV scores range from –10 to 10). Logit is generally suitable for variation in a dependent variable that does not exceed 4–5 values. Robust standard errors are used to fix heteroscedasticity. The *Cooperative Duration Hypothesis* (H_2) is estimated using duration/survival analysis, to determine the probability of a democratic reversal. Originally developed in biometrics and commonly used to determine patient survival rates, the duration model assesses the differences in democratic survival times among nations (Box-Steffensmeier and Jones 2004) and is concerned with analyzing the time to the occurrence of an event (i.e., a democratic breakdown which involves the qualitative change in the political order of a nation). Survival analysis, applied to our model, is the study of the survival of democratic forms of government.

OLS is not suitable for analyzing survival because the distributions of the residuals are assumed to be normal. However, for many events the assumed normality of time-to-event is unreasonable. For example, it is unreasonable to assume that democratic survival times are normally distributed across transition type and country. Survival analysis makes a substitution for the normality assumption characterized by OLS with something more appropriate for the problem at hand (Cleves *et al.* 2008, 2). The dependent variable used in survival analysis is dichotomous (i.e., either the country survived as a democracy or it reverted to authoritarianism). Feng and Zak (1999, 172) note,

The specification of the estimation as a hazard function advances the statistical methodology used in estimating democratic transitions. Because this method is robust statistically for the estimation of a limited dependent variable, the results ... are more meaningful than using, say, logit estimation.

Analysis

The empirical results provide strong supporting confirmation of the theory. Table 2 presents the OLS estimation of H_1. The *Cooperative Quality Hypothesis* is overwhelmingly confirmed.[10] Specifically, cooperative transitions result in higher average levels of democracy in the posttransitional phase compared to transition by conversion. Transition by cooperation is associated with higher Polity IV scores at years 4–6, 7–10 and 1–10 after the transition and the results are significant at the 0.01 level. During the first three years after a transition, no discernable pattern of democratic success exists. The first few years after a transition are likely to be characterized by greater uncertainty than later years. The reason for this is logical. In the immediate posttransitional stage, parties and elites attempt to position themselves to make the greatest gains in the new political environment, bargaining and staging for positions that will benefit them the most. Only after a few years of surviving as a democracy can a trajectory be established that either shows steady progress towards (or away from) democracy.

Beginning with years 4–6, the time when the second democratic national elections are typically held, cooperative transitions are associated with Polity IV scores that are 3.14 points higher than transition by conversion. In years 7–10, the stage at which a democracy is either beginning to flourish or backslide,

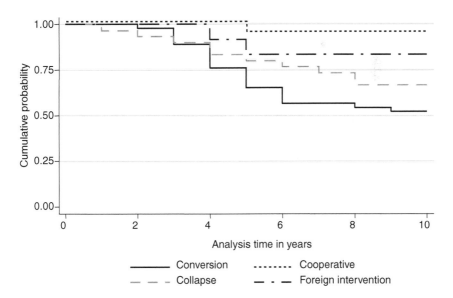

Figure 4.2 Kaplan–Meier survival estimates, by transition type.

Table 4.2 OLS regression for democratic quality – ten years after transition (robust standard errors in parentheses)

Independent variables	(1) PY1–3	(2) PY4–6	(3) PY7–10	(4) PY1–10
TRANSITION TYPE				
• Conversion	—	—	—	—
• Cooperative	0.547 (.397)	3.14*** (.844)	4.51*** (1.13)	2.91*** (0.726)
• Collapse	−0.850 (0.578)	2.03* (1.11)	1.63 (1.51)	1.02 (0.934)
• Foreign intervention	0.483 (0.797)	2.02* (1.04)	3.86** (1.90)	1.32 (1.24)
REGION				
• Europe	1.11 (0.710)	0.062 (1.07)	0.789 (2.07)	0.878 (1.21)
• North Africa and Middle East	1.25 (.789)	−1.50 (1.93)	−2.23 (2.96)	−0.636 (1.67)
• South America	0.080 (0.569)	−0.912 (1.12)	−0.223 (2.05)	−0.506 (1.19)
• Asia and Pacific	0.248 (0.727)	−1.02 (1.11)	−0.408 (2.04)	−0.755 (1.27)
• Sub-Saharan Africa	0.002 (0.664)	−1.32 (1.27)	−3.32 (2.11)	−2.13* (1.24)
INSTITUTIONAL CHOICE				
• Parliamentary	0.614 (0.543)	0.627 (0.985)	−0.903 (1.32)	−0.320 (0.866)
• Mixed	0.714 (0.521)	0.261 (1.05)	−0.231 (1.48)	0.359 (0.969)
PRIOR REGIME TYPE				
• Single party	−1.60** (0.720)	−1.75 (1.17)	−0.502 (1.67)	−1.31 (1.11)
• Personalistic	−0.608 (0.561)	−1.31 (1.26)	0.450 (1.56)	−0.598 (1.06)
• Previous colony	0.062 (0.709)	−0.138 (1.35)	0.854 (1.92)	0.000
PRIOR DEMOCRATIC HISTORY				
• Yes	0.143 (0.378)	−0.221 (.827)	−0.690 (1.18)	−0.476 (0.727)
PER CAPITA GDP	0.000153** (0.000076)	0.000221 (0.000148)	0.00039*** (0.00014)	0.000254** (0.00012)
GDP GROWTH RATE	1.17 (1.51)	8.37 (4.26)*	4.06 (5.32)	2.57* (0.985)
Constant robust standard rror	6.38*** (0.656)	4.93*** (1.06)	2.32 (2.14)	4.44*** (1.14)
R²	0.32	0.31	0.36	0.40
N	111	113	112	108

Notes
Significance levels: *** <0.01; ** <0.05; * <0.10 (two-tailed tests).
Model 1 reflects the year 1, 2, 3 Polity average of the dependent variable.
Model 2 reflects the year 4, 5, 6 Polity average of the dependent variable.
Model 3 reflects the year 7, 8, 9, 10 Polity average of the dependent variable.
Model 4 reflects the 10- year Polity average of the dependent variable.
Models 1–4 use conversion as the baseline category of the dependent variable. Dataset includes all democratic transitions since 1900.

cooperative transitions are associated with Polity IV scores that are 4.51 points higher than conversion. Across the ten-year average, the Polity scores for cooperative transitions are approximately 3 points higher than transition by conversion. Substantively, this can represent the difference between a democratic regime and an autocratic one (e.g., a Polity score of 4 is considered a soft authoritarian regime while a 7 is considered a democratic polity). On the Polity IV scale, this represents a 15 percent higher rating.

The results also show foreign intervention to be significant at the .10 level at years 4–6 and significant at the0 .05 level at years 7–10. We believe the result is driven by World War II interventions and their high Polity ratings after the war. As a result, we re-run the analysis and control for World War II (see Appendix B – robustness check 3). The results confirm that foreign interventions are driven by the success of WWII cases. When controlling for WWII, the significance of foreign intervention goes away completely while the results for cooperative transitions increase slightly.

Our results lend partial support to the argument that pacted transitions are more likely to result in consolidated democracies than other transition types

Table 4.3 Duration analysis for democratic longevity – ten years after transition

Independent variables	Parameter estimate (hazard ratio)	Robust standard error	Risk ratio (z)	P
TRANSITION TYPE				
• Conversion	–	–	–	–
• Cooperative	0.059	0.055	–3.02***	0.003
• Collapse	0.434	0.259	–1.40	0.162
• Foreign intervention	0.386	0.293	–1.25	0.211
INSTITUTIONAL CHOICE				
• Parliamentary	4.48	2.15	3.13***	0.002
• Mixed	2.72	1.72	1.58	0.114
PRIOR REGIME TYPE				
• Single party	0.937	0.487	–0.12	0.901
• Personalistic	0.533	0.387	–0.87	0.387
• Colonial history	0.259	0.136	–2.56**	0.010
PRIOR DEMOCRATIC HISTORY				
• Yes	0.735	0.307	–0.74	0.462
PER CAPITA GDP	0.999	0.0002	–2.56**	0.010
GDP GROWTH RATE	222	239	–1.40	0.163

Notes
Number of subjects: 107.
Number of failures: 31.
Time at risk=904.
Wald Chi Squared: 47.14.
Significance levels: *** <0.01; ** <0.05; * <0.10.
The model uses conversion as the baseline transition category and reflects the GDP per capita average over ten years, in addition to ten-year GDP growth rate.

(O'Donnell and Schmitter 1986; Karl 1990; Karl and Schmitter 1991). As discussed earlier, it is problematic to lump all pacts into one category but is necessary to distinguish who holds the power advantage in the pact. For example, O'Donnell and Schmitter (1986) claim that "Pacts ... are desirable [and] enhance the probability that the process will lead to a viable political democracy" (39). Yet, pact by conversion is the most detrimental to democracy, with an almost 50 percent failure rate (see Table 1.1). In part, this is attributable to the fact that converted transitions, while containing certain elements of pacts, also contain competition-suppressing features that may override any beneficial features of the cooperative environment that pacts are supposed to promote. Where the incumbents hold a distinct power advantage, they are less likely to negotiate with the opposition, which potentially poisons the atmosphere of cooperation that defines successful pacts. O'Donnell and Schmitter make an important point – that pacts "are meant to accommodate 'vital interests' and, therefore, facilitate the installation of democracy" (1080). Under cooperative transitions this is precisely what happens; it is not clear that converted transitions accommodate vital interests to the extent needed for democracy to succeed.

Our results lend less support to Karl (1987), Przeworski (1991) and Hagopian (1996), who argue that pacted transitions are characterized by the suppression of competition. Perhaps these scholars were focusing on incumbent-led pacts, which explains why pacts turn into

> ...cartels that restrict competition, bar access, and distribute the benefits of political power among the insiders. Democracy would then turn into a private project of leaders of some political parties and corporatist associations, an oligopoly in which leaders of some organizations collude to prevent outsiders from entering.
>
> (Przeworski 1991, 90–91)

As previously noted, Karl (1987) suggests that pacts tend to demobilize new social forces and circumscribe the participation of certain actors in the future, thereby producing a "frozen democracy" (88).

Region, institutional choice and prior regime type appear to exert little influence on democratic success. Sub-Saharan Africa, over the ten-year Polity average, is associated with a Polity IV score that is –2.13 points lower than the baseline category, North America, and is significant at the 0.10 level. Institutional choice, whether presidential, parliamentary or mixed, shows no degree of significance. Prior regime type is significant at the 0.05 level at years 1–3, with single party regimes displaying –1.60 Polity points lower than military regimes. No other prior regime type reaches statistically significant levels.

Consistent with the literature, per capita GDP is highly significant; the wealthier a country, the higher its Polity IV score. The implications are important. Przeworski *et al.* (2000) argues that countries with higher levels of GDP per capita remain democratic; the results in the current study clearly support this. Similarly, Epstein *et al.* (2006) empirically show that higher per capita GDP reduces the probability that countries will abandon democracy (564). GDP growth rates also exert a strong effect on the ten-year average Polity IV rating. Intuitively, we expect democracies that are associated with robust economic growth to provide legitimacy to a new democratic regime, thereby increasing the strength of the democracy.

While the regression results indicate cooperative transitions are associated with higher levels of democracy in the post-transitional stage, we next test H_2, the *Cooperative Quality Hypothesis*, to determine the effect of mode of transition on democratic duration using survival analysis (Table 4.3). Survival analysis is concerned with studying the time between entry to the study (in this case, the first democratic election) and a subsequent event (democratic death, previously defined as when the Polity IV score drops below a 5). Censored survival times are also utilized if the event of interest does not occur for a nation-state during the study period. In interpreting hazard models a positive sign on the coefficient indicates that the hazard (risk of a democratic death) is higher. Alternatively, a negative coefficient implies a better prognosis (the risk of reversal is reduced). In Table 4.3, the direction of the coefficient is indicated by the z-score; however, we do not list actual coefficients but rather the hazard ratio for ease of interpretation. To interpret hazard scores, subtract the hazard ratio from 1; the difference is the reduction in hazard (e.g., a hazard ratio of 0.2 means that Group 1 has an 80 percent smaller hazard than the baseline category). Thus, the smaller the hazard ratio, the greater the reduction in risk.

Compared to the baseline category (conversion), cooperative pacts have a 94 percent lower risk (1-0.059) of democratic death and the finding is statistically significant at the 0.01 level. This lends strong supporting evidence to H_1 – not only are cooperative transitions associated with higher levels of democracy, they also last longer. Other significant variables include GDP per capita with a very strong effect (a one-unit change in GDP is associated with a 1 percent decrease in reversion – this finding is consistent with the regression results and with Lipset's (1959) statement that "the more well-to-do a nation, the greater the chances that it will sustain democracy" (75). Parliamentary systems revert at a greater rate than presidential regimes and prior colonial regimes survive longer than when the authoritarian regime was militaristic, since stronger military regimes imply greater autonomy of the military, which can be detrimental to democracy. Although we had no expected direction of the coefficient for institutional choice, we are somewhat surprised by the magnitude of the failure rate of parliamentary regimes compared to presidential regimes. Additional research will be needed to fully understand this occurrence.

The Kaplan–Meier (Figure 4.2) plot estimates the survivor function and serves as a step function (the estimated survival probabilities are constant between adjacent reversal times and only decrease at each democratic death). The Kaplan–Meier function demonstrates how transition by collapse and conversion start to show immediate reversions to dictatorship (in some cases within the first two years), while cooperative transitions experience no reversions until approximately year 5. Cooperative transitions largely stabilize at that point and remain democratic while transition by collapse and conversion are characterized by a steady step-wise decline in democracy.

Based on the regression and duration analysis results, we find strong supporting evidence that transition by cooperative pact is conducive to democracy. Alternatively, transition by conversion appears detrimental to one-half of the democracies that transition through this method. Thus, not all negotiated transitions are equal – the important difference is where the balance of power lies. Where opposition groups hold a power advantage, democracy is more likely to flourish. When incumbents hold a power advantage they tend to design electoral rules and other institutions that guarantee their continued success and this impedes democracy. The impediment lies in the notion that excluded groups will both feel frustrated by their lack of ability to push the nation towards democracy and their inability to participate in the reformed system of government.

The goal of H_1 and H_2 is to demonstrate the independent effects that the mode of transition has on democratic success. In Model II, we explore the hypotheses put forth by Geddes (1999) in her important work on prior regime type. Geddes suggests that military regimes, on average, do not last as long as other types of regimes and are more likely to negotiate their extrications and will be followed by competitive political systems. Geddes notes that they are less likely to end in coups, popular uprising, armed insurgency, revolution, invasion, or assassination. In support of this finding Svolik (2008) argues, "…democracies that were preceded by a military dictatorship face significantly lower chances of becoming consolidated" (162). Personalist regimes, in contrast, are more likely than other types to end in violence and upheaval and personal dictators rarely leave office voluntarily. Their ends are also more likely to be precipitated by the death of the dictator or through foreign pressure, and they are more likely to be followed by some new form of authoritarianism. Single party regimes last the longest, but when uncontrollable popular opposition signals that the end is near, like the military, they negotiate the transition.

First, Geddes argues military regimes negotiate their way out of power. In the present study, this implies that military regimes will either exit through a conversion or cooperative transition as stated in H_3 (*Peaceful Military Transition Hypothesis*). It seems counterintuitive that regimes built and maintained by force would relinquish power without a struggle, thus we expect military regimes to transition through violence rather than leave office voluntarily. Table 4.4 empirically provides challenging results to Geddes' findings by showing that military regimes do not transfer power peacefully; however, they are more likely to transfer through foreign intervention with results significant at the 0.05 level. Compared to personalistic regimes, they are almost three times as likely to be overthrown by a foreign invader.

Next, Geddes posits that personalistic regimes are more likely to transition through a collapse or foreign intervention as stated in H_4 (*Violent Personalistic Transition Hypothesis*). We do not find support for this hypothesis. It appears that personalistic regimes show no discernable transitional type pattern. Finally, Geddes asserts that single party regimes are more likely to result in either a

Table 4.4 Multinomial logistic regression results of prior regime type on transition type (robust standard errors)

Transition type	Conversion	Cooperative	Foreign intervention
PRIOR REGIME TYPE			
• Personalistic	—	—	—
• Military	−0.571 (0.0.938)	−1.753* (1.004)	2.759** (1.330)
• Single party	2.539** (1.045)	2.054** (0.9222)	−31.817*** (1.311)
• Colonialism	0.643 (0.773)	−0.118 (0.792)	0.389 (1.895)
REGION			
• Europe	−3.034** (1.545)	−1.690 (1.610)	0.087 (1.6140
• North Africa and Middle East	−2.102 (1.609)	−36.2688*** (1.612)	−35.577*** (1.615)
• South America	−0.076 (1.401)	−0.130 (1.546)	−35.540*** (1.175)
• Asia and Pacific	−1.502 (1.494)	−0.651 (1.615)	−1.213 (1.349)
• Sub-Saharan Africa	0.001 (1.471)	0.229 (1.589)	−33.907*** (1.482)
PRIOR DEMOCRATIC HISTORY			
• Yes	0.344 (0.687)	−0.534 (0.694)	−0.248 (1.589)
Constant robust standard error R^2 N	1.062 (1.513) 0.279 122	1.259 (1.618) 0.279 122	−1.575 (1.555) 0.279 122

Notes
Significance levels: *** <0.01; ** <0.05; * <0.10 (two-tailed tests).
Dependent variable = prior regime type; explanatory variable = transition type.
Dataset includes all democratic transitions since 1900.

cooperative or conversion transition as stated in H$_5$ (*Peaceful Single Party Regime Transition*). This suggests that single party regimes are likely to transition peacefully, either through the negotiated mechanisms of conversion or cooperation, and the results strongly indicate this is the case at the 0.05 level. Having a prior regime type of single party versus personalistic increases the long odds of transitioning by conversion or cooperation. Alternatively, single party regimes have decreased log odds of transitioning by foreign intervention with results highly significant at the 0.01 level. Here Geddes' argument holds and it is necessary to further our analysis to determine the influence of single party regimes on democratic quality and duration.

In examining the effect of transition type on region the following is noted. First, North Africa and the Middle East, South America and Sub-Saharan Africa are not likely to transition through foreign intervention with results significant at the 0.01 level. This is clearly supported by the dataset – the majority of foreign interventions occurred in World War II; later interventions included Haiti and Panama. North Africa and the Middle East are also not likely to transition through cooperative pact, while Europe is less likely to transition by conversion. In all, there appears to be no discernable pattern that dictates transition type by region. Prior democratic history also shows no significance for any transition type.

In Tables 4.5 and 4.6., we model prior regime type as the explanatory variable and democratic quality and duration as the dependent variable to complete our analyses of Geddes' argument. To restate, Geddes posits that militaristic and single party regimes negotiate their exit. We also find strong support that single party regimes engage in negotiated transitions; however, military regimes tend to transition violently. The logical extension of Geddes argument concerning single party regimes is that they should result in higher levels of democracy and last longer (assuming the majority of these transitions are cooperative in nature; however, Geddes does not make this distinction. The premise of her argument is that single party regimes negotiate the transition to democracy but, as we have shown, the balance of power is important for sustainable democracy). Over a ten-year average, the regression results indicate that single party regimes do not demonstrate higher levels of democracy compared to other prior regime types. In fact, the results indicate that none of the prior regime types exert a strong influence on democratic quality ratings over a ten-year average, with only modest effects for single party and personalistic regimes in years 1–3 in the posttransitional phase. In Table 4.6., we model prior regime type on democratic duration. The results clearly indicate that there are no discernable patterns that indicate prior regime type influences the duration of democracy.

The impact of prior regime type in determining mode of transition is unclear at best. The only discernable pattern is that single party regimes tend to transition peacefully. In our dataset, 14 out of 46 converted transitions are single party regimes, and 17 out of 36 are cooperative transitions. However, we fail to see a statistical relationship that indicates single party regimes are associated with greater democratic quality and duration. Thus, it appears that prior regime

Table 4.5 OLS results for democratic quality – prior regime type (robust standard errors)

Independent variable	(1) PY1–3	(2) PY4–6	(3) PY7–10	(4) PY1–10
PRIOR REGIME TYPE				
• Military	–	–	–	–
• Single party	−1.085** (0.490)	−0.956 (0.909)	0.272 (1.305)	−0.496 (0.854)
• Personalistic	−0.716 (0.417)*	−1.367 (1.033)	−0.304 (1.363)	−0.683 (0.876)
• Prior colony	−0.107 (0.426)	−0.347 (0.967)	−0.445 (1.512)	−0.248 (0.912)
Constant robust standard Error	7.702*** (0.300)	6.936*** (0.667)	5.130*** (0.992) 0.0027	6.41*** (0.63)
R^2	0.060	0.019	121	0.0057
N	123	121	–	123

Notes
Significance levels: *** <.01; ** <.05; * <0.10.
The model uses military as the baseline prior regime type category.

Table 4.6 Duration analysis results – prior regime type (robust standard errors)

Independent variable	Parameter estimate (hazard ratio)	Robust standard error	Risk ratio (z)	P
PRIOR REGIME TYPE				
• Military	–	–	–	–
• Single party	1.111	0.488	0.24	0.810
• Personalistic	0.823	0.443	–0.36	0.718
• Prior colony	1.511	0.634	0.98	0.325

Notes
N = 121.
Wald Chi Squared = 1.71.
Significance levels: *** <.01; ** <.05; * <.10.
The model uses military as baseline prior regime type category.

type does not have a causal link with democratic quality and longevity. Yet, the mode of transition clearly does. The mechanisms that emerge from the actual transition contain the elements necessary for successful democracy and this is independent of the nature of the prior regime type. In other words, successful democratization is not an artifact of the nature of the prior regime but rather linked to the mechanisms at play during the transitional process. For any prior regime type (militaristic, personalistic and single party) that engages in coopera-tive transitions, this increases their chance of succeeding at democracy. For example, if a military regime displays characteristics of a cooperative transition then it is likely to succeed; if a single party regime displays non-cooperative properties, chances are it will not be successful.

Notes

1 We use 1900 as the cut-off point because it is difficult to obtain reliable data on eco-nomic and democratic quality ratings prior to that year. Further, the number of transi-tioning states prior to 1900 is relatively small.
2 See Figure 3.2 "Modes of transition, a unified approach."
3 1998 is the cut-off point to allow for ten years of Polity measurement.
4 For example, in 1986 the Philippines were coded by Polity as a –88, which signifies "transition": the period during which new institutions are planned etc. Currently Iraq and Afghanistan are coded as –66, which signifies "interruption," typically meaning foreign occupation. Not all transitioning states reflect interruption Polity scores; however, when they do we start to measure democracy once they emerge from this period and obtain actual democratic Polity scores.
5 Our standard for breakdown is when the Polity score drops three or more points from one year to the next. This rule is consistent with Polity IV, which uses a three-point change to indicate a regime transition.
6 Dahl (1990) notes that, except in Uruguay, democracy has never been internally sub-verted in any nation where it has survived for 20 years.
7 In this study we are concerned with economic growth as a causal factor in the survival of democracy, not economic growth as a causal factor in the transition to democracy.
8 Last updated October 2008.

9 The posttransitional phase refers to the period immediately after the first national democratic election is held. In general, the posttransitional phase ends as democracy deepens or destructs if the nation returns to dictatorship.

10 Transition by conversion is used as the baseline category.

References

Beetham David, Sarah Bracking, Iain Kearton, Nalini Vittal and Stuart Weir. 2002., eds. *The State of Democracy: Democarcy Assessments in Eight Nations arouind the World*. The Hague: Kluwer Law International: 100–103.

Box-Steffensmeier, Janet M. and Bradford S. Jones. 2004. *Timing and Political Change: Event History Modeling in Political Science*. Ann Arbor: University of Michigan Press.

Cheibub, Jose Antonio. 2007. *Presidentialism, Parliamentarism, and Democracy*. Cambridge: Cambridge University Press.

Cleves, M. William W. Gould, Roberto G. Gutierrz and Yulia Marchenko. 2008. *An Introduction to Survival Analysis Using Stata*. 2nd edition. Stata Press.

Dahl, Robert A. 1998. *On Democracy*. New Haven: Yale University Press.

Diamond, Larry. 1992. "Economic Development and Democracy Reconsidered." In *Reexamining Democracy*, ed. Gary Marks and Larry Diamond. Newbury Park: SAGE, 93–139.

Epstein, David L., Robert Bates, Jack Goldstone, Ida Kristensen and Sharyn O'Halloran. 2006. "Democratic Transitions." *American Journal of Political Science* 50(3): 551–569.

Evans, Geoffrey and Stephen Whitefield. 1995. "The Politics and Economics of Democratic Commitment: Support for Democracy in Transition Societies." *British Journal of Political Science* 25(4): 485–514.

Feng, Yi and Paul J. Zak. 1999. "The Determinants of Democratic Transitions." *The Journal of Conflict Resolution* 43(2): 162–177.

Gasiorowski, Mark. 1996. "An Overview of the Political Regime Dataset." *Comparative Political Studies* 29(4): 469:83.

Gasiorowski, Mark and Timothy Power. 1997. "Institutional Design and Democratic Consolidation in the Third World." *Comparative Political Studies* 30: 123–155.

Gates, Scott, Håvard Hegre, Mark P. Jones and Håvard Strand. 2006. "Institutional Inconsistency and Political Instability: Polity Duration, 1800–2000." *American Journal of Political Science* 50(4): 893–908.

Geddes, Barbara. 1999. "Authoritarian Breakdown: Empirical Test of a Game Theoretic Approach." *Paper prepared for the annual meeting of the American Political Science Association*, Atlanta, Georgia.

Gurr, Ted Robert. 1974. "Persistence and Change in Political Systems 1800–1971." *American Political Science Review* 68: 1482–1504.

Hagopian, Frances. 1996. *Traditional Politics and Regime Change in Brazil*. New York: Cambridge University Press.

Hartman, John and Wey Hsiao. 1988. "Inequality and Violence: Issues of Theory and Measurement in Muller." *American Sociological Review* 53: 794–800.

Hermens, F.A. 1941. *Democracy or Anarchy: A Study of Proportional Representation*. Notre Dame: Notre Dame Press.

Huntington, Samuel P. 1991. *The Third Wave: Democratization in the Late Twentieth Century*. Norman: University of Oklahoma Press.

Karl, Terry Lynn. 1987. "Petroleum and Political Pacts." *Latin American Research Review* 22: 63–94.

Karl, Terry Lynn. 1990. "Dilemmas of Democratization in Latin America." *Comparative Politics* 23 (1): 1–22

Karl, Terry Lynn and Philippe C. Schmitter. 1991. "Modes of transition in Latin America, Southern and Eastern Europe." *International Social Science Journal* 128: 269–284.

Linz, Juan. 1978. "Crisis Breakdown and Reequilibration." In *The Breakdown of Democratic Regimes*, ed. Juan J. Linz and Alfred Stepan. Baltimore and London: The Johns Hopkins University Press.

Linz, Juan. 1990. "The Perils of Presidentialism." *Journal of Democracy* (Winter): 51:69.

Linz, Juan J. 1994. "Presidential or Parliamentary Democracy: Does It Make a Difference?" In *The Failure of Presidential Democracy*, ed. Juan J. Linz and Arturo Valenzuela, eds. Baltimore: Johns Hopkins University Press, 3–87.

Lipset, Seymour Martin. 1959. "Some Social Requisites of Democracy: Economic Development and Political Legitimacy." *American Political Science Review* 5: 69–105.

Mainwaring, Scott. 1993. "Presidentialism, Multipartism, and Democracy: The Difficult Combination." *Comparative Political Studies* 26: 198–228.

Mainwaring, Scott and Matthew Shugart, eds. 1997. *Presidentialism and Democracy in Latin America.* Cambridge: Cambridge University Press.

Mainwaring, Scott and Aníbal Pérez-Liñán. 2005. "Latin American Democratization since 1978: Democratic Transitions, Breakdowns, and Erosions." In *The Third Wave of Democratization in Latin America: Advances and Setbacks*, ed. Hagopian and Mainwaring. New York: Cambridge University Press.

Marshall, G., Keith Jaggers and Ted Robert Gurr. 2007. Polity IV Project: Political Regime Characteristics and Transitions, 1800–2007. *www.systemicpeace.org/polity/polity4.htm* (accessed on March 31, 2008).

Munck, Gerardo L. and Carol Skalnik Leff. 1997. "Modes of Transition and Democratization: South American and Eastern Europe in Comparative Perspective." *Comparative Politics* 29: 343–362.

Nagle, John D. 1985. *Introduction to Comparative Politics: Political Systems and Performance in Three Worlds.* Chicago, Illinois: Nelson-Hall Publishers.

O'Donnell, Guillermo and Philippe Schmitter. 1986. *Transitions from Authoritarian Rule: Tentative Conclusions about Uncertain Democracies.* Baltimore: The Johns Hopkins University Press.

Polity IV Project. 2006. *Polity IV Dataset. [Computer file; version p4v2000]* College Park, MD: Center for International Development and Conflict Management, University of Maryland.

Przeworski, Adam. 1991. *Democracy and the Market.* New York: Cambridge University Press.

Przeworski, Adam and Fernando Limongi. 1997. "Modernization: Theories and Facts." *World Politics* 49: 155–183.

Przeworski, Adam, Michael Alvarez, Jose Antonio Cheibub and Fernando Limongi. 2000. *Democracy and Development: Political Institutions and Well-Being in the World, 1950–1990.* New York: Cambridge University Press.

Reich, G. 2002. "Categorizing Political Regimes: New Data for Old Problems." *Democratization* 9: 1–24.

Rueschemeyer, Dietrich. 1991. "Different Methods, Contradictory Results? Research on Development and Democracy." *International Journal of Comparative Sociology* 32: 9–38.

Scoble, Harry M. and Laurie S. Wiseberg 1981. "Problems of Comparative Research on Human Rights." In *Global Human Rights: Public Policies, Comparative Measures, and NGO Strategies*, ed. Ved P. Nanda, James R. Scarritt and George W. Shepherd, Jr. Boulder, Colorado: Westview Press.

Share, Donald and Scott Mainwaring. 1986. "Transitions through transaction: democratization in Brazil and Spain." In *Political liberalization in Brazil: Dynamics, Dilemmas and Future Prospects*, ed. Wayne Selcher. Boulder: Westview, 175–215.

Stepan, Alfred and Cindy Skach. 1993. "Constitutional Frameworks and Democratic Consolidation: Parliamentarism and Presidentialism." *World Politics* 46: 1–22.

Svolik, Milan. 2008. "Authoritarian Reversals and Democratic Consolidation." *American Political Science Review* 102(2): 153–168.

Ward, Michael D. and Kristian S. Gleditsch. 1998 "Democratizing for Peace." *American Political Science Review* 92(1): 52–62.

Wejnert, Barbara. 2005. "Diffusion, Development, and Democracy, 1800–1999." *American Sociological Review* 70(1): 53–81.

5 Democratic prospects

Understanding that the mode of transition influences the quality and duration of a democracy is practically useful because this knowledge can be applied to future transitioning states. Many nations in Asia, the Middle East and Africa are yet to make the transition to democracy as they continue to be held in the grip of repressive authoritarian regimes. In this chapter, we examine the prospects for successful democracy through predicted value probability analysis in various countries that have recently initiated a process of transition and also provide some case studies on the mode of transition in Iraq, Tunisia, Egypt, Libya, Yemen and China, a country with the possibility of transitioning in the future.

The usefulness of the predicted value probabilities is that they provide insight into how the explanatory variables impact the dependent variable, the quality and strength of democracy as measured through Polity IV scores. In the Middle East and North Africa, region has historically been a hindrance to democratization, perhaps due to the nature of rentier states. Prior regime type also exerts a negative influence on the prospects for successful democracy. The single party regime appears to provide a larger obstacle than if the prior regime was personalistic. Theories abound regarding this and future research is needed to flesh these ideas out. As expected, per capita GDP and growth rates exert a strong positive influence on the prospects for creating successful democracy. High levels of growth can bring about legitimacy to a new regime and this legitimacy is essential to the survivability of democratic government.

We start our discussion by examining Iraq, liberated from the brutal Hussein regime through a coalition led by the United States (i.e., foreign intervention) in 2003. Next, we turn to four countries of the Arab Spring – Tunisia, Egypt, Libya and Yemen – all of which started a process of liberalization through regime change. At the time of this writing, it appears the directions of these transitions are towards democracy though this is tenuous at best and each country faces numerous obstacles to successful democratization. Whereas negotiations characterize peaceful transitions, the violent transitional processes of collapse and foreign intervention reflect a lack of, or breakdown in, negotiations with the incumbent regime and frequently involve bloodshed; the power disparities in these transitions are significant. Unless a more powerful opposition can force the hand of a weak incumbent government to transition the nation-state away from dictatorship, the opposition's use of force to affect political change is a necessity. In these instances, the opposition will unite and initiate regime overthrow through violence as occurred in Libya while relatively peaceful transitions occurred in Tunisia, Egypt and Yemen. While these transitions all started "from below" they were only able to proceed with help from the establishment. Therefore, we see "cooperative" features in many of these transitions. We conclude with an assessment of a potential peaceful democratic transition in the People's Republic of China, examining two possible modes of regime change in the future – conversion and cooperative.

Iraq

Iraq was liberated from the regime of Saddam Hussein by coalition forces led by the U.S. and Great Britain in March of 2003. Ten years later, the country continues to struggle in its quest to become a fully functioning democratic state. A key question in Iraq is whether or not it is possible to impose democracy upon a country. While foreign interventions were largely successful in restoring democracy during World War II, the circumstances surrounding those liberations were quite different from what occurred in Iraq. Can foreign intervention provide the impetus for successful democratization?

As discussed in preceding chapters, the process of democratizing a country can be viewed on a continuum. Democratization involves three steps: (1) the removal of the authoritarian regime; (2) installation of a democratic regime; and (3) the consolidation, or long-term sustainability, of the democratic regime. In Iraq, where internal prerequisites failed to bring regime change or start the process of democratization, foreign intervention was an important, causal factor contributing to the removal of the authoritarian regime (step 1) and the installation of a democratic regime (step 2). In the asence of internal prerequisites to cause regime change, the prospects for democratizing Iraq are directly tied to the success of foreign intervention in overthrowing the target regime and installing a democratic government. Democratic sustainability is then developed through subsequent U.S. and international involvement in reconstruction during the formative transitional phase, and the target state's ability to improve socioeconomic conditions, create strong democratic institutions and increase the rule of law, which ultimately provides legitimacy to the new government.

From early on, numerous scholars expressed pessimism about the likelihood of Iraq building a viable, democratic regime after Saddam Hussein (Diamond 2003, 2005; Lawson and Thacker 2003). It is deemed that democracy is likely to fail as Iraq does not possess the necessary prerequisites for constructing and maintaining a stable democratic system, and because external factors are secondary to internal factors in creating democracy (Lowenthal 1991). Internal factors include socioeconomic, political, cultural and historical variables that help mold the forces responsible for the emergence and stabilization of democratic structures.

How have countries faired when the transitional mode to democracy have occurred through *foreign intervention*, in particular by the United States military? Scholars have posited intervention to mean the direct or indirect use of military force for the purpose of "changing or preserving the structure of political authority in the target society" (Rosenau 1969, 161); and "a political use of military force involving ground troops of either the U.S. Army or Marine Corps in an active attempt to influence the behavior of other nations" (Blechman and Kaplan 1978).

Some scholars have argued that U.S. efforts to export democracy through military intervention have been "negligible, often counterproductive, and only occasionally positive" (Lowenthal 1991: 243). They assert that democracy cannot be coercively imposed by foreign governments and that there is an inherent contradiction in forcing states to be free (Herman and Brodhead 1984; Karl 1990; Whitehead 1991). Recent studies, however, suggest that overt U.S. military interventions have the positive effect of leaving targeted states more liberal than they were prior to intervention (Hermann and Kegley 1998; Meernik 1996). Nations which experienced U.S. military intervention are 15 percent more likely to make democratic gains (Meernik 1996, 396). Meernik also found that when a U.S. president declares democracy as the goal of intervention, and when the U.S. government is opposed to the targeted regime, democratization is more likely to be promoted. With Iraq, U.S. President George W. Bush (2003) stated the goal of U.S. military intervention was to "free its people" and to help "Iraqis achieve a united, stable and free country."[1]

Peceny (1999) studied the impact "of the most prominent type of pro-liberalization policy pursued during military intervention: the promotion of free and fair elections in targeted states" (550). By examining a dataset consisting of those countries where the United States actively promoted free and fair election during military interventions (direct and indirect interventions) between 1889 and 1993, Peceny shows a positive and statistically significant impact on democracy. It is the promotion of free and fair elections during intervention, rather than the intervention itself that has the most powerful impact on democratization in target states (Peceny 1999: 552). However, without the intervention, the process of liberalization could not otherwise begin.

Iraq contains some 143 to 350 billion barrels of oil reserves in addition to 110 trillion cubic feet of natural gas (EIA 2012). The large disparity in estimates is due to the decades of war and unrest that has plagued Iraq. Additionally, many of Iraq's oil wells are antiquated and not operating at full capacity.

According to the U.S. Energy Information Administration (EIA 2012) Iraq was the world's twelfth largest oil producer in 2009, and has the world's fourth largest proven petroleum reserves after Saudi Arabia, Canada and Iran. It is believed that just a fraction of Iraq's known fields are in development and producing. The EIA (2012) also indicates that "Iraq may be one of the few places left where vast reserves, proven and unknown, have barely been exploited." According to the *Oil and Gas Journal*, Iraq's proven natural gas reserves are 112 trillion cubic feet (Tcf), the tenth largest in the world.

As technology and infrastructure is improved, increases in oil production will provide Iraq with additional revenue and rising incomes, but herein lies some of Iraq's greatest obstacles in its transformation along with that of other oil-rich states in the Middle East, that of the "resource curse," which holds that states rich in natural resources tend to experience relatively low levels of economic growth, and the fact that such states are prone to authoritarian politics, known as "rentierism." In many cases, natural-resource-abundant economies grow at a slow pace and are prone to being development failures (Sachs and Warner 1995; Gylfason 2001). During the last two centuries, countries rich in natural resources, such as Russia, Nigeria and Venezuela, have experienced relatively low levels of growth. In contrast, countries with limited access to natural resources, such as Japan, Hong Kong, Korea, Singapore and Switzerland, experienced remarkably high economic growth rates. Since natural resources provide a substantial source of income, and this revenue can be converted to capital improvement projects, such as infrastructure modernization, and education and health services, there is no obvious reason why natural resources frustrate economic growth, as experienced by many resource-rich countries.

Studies show, on average, natural resources have a negative impact on growth when considered in isolation, but a positive impact when other explanatory variables, such as corruption, investments, openness, terms of trade and schooling are included (Papyrakis and Gerlagh 2003). That is, natural resources seem to stimulate growth, but only under certain conditions. Thus, it is essential to control for indirect, adverse effects. A natural resource economy that suffers from corruption, low investments, protectionist measures, a deteriorating terms of trade and low educational standards probably will not benefit from its natural wealth. When governments attenuate the negative factors through which natural resources harm growth, they can benefit from natural wealth. Resource-abundant countries, such as Norway and Iceland, have experienced remarkable and sustained growth rates. When comparing successful cases (Norway and Iceland) to failures (Russia, Venezuela and Nigeria), the more stable democracies have avoided the resource curse. Presumably, this is due to the strength of democratic institutions in those countries, including a strong rule of law. Successful democratization can curb adverse effects, and is contingent upon controlling corruption through institutional engineering.

The problem of rentier states is of equal concern (Al-Naqeeb 1990; Adbulla 1999). Since the regime derives a large portion of its revenue from external rents and relies less on citizens' taxes, its accountability to the populace is diminished and citizens' leverage of the state is small. In general, citizens in many of the Arab Middle East countries are not obligated to make substantial financial contributions to the state and are dependent, either directly or indirectly, on government expenditures. While modernization theory suggests greater levels of economic development propel societies toward democracy, it fails to explain the democracy deficit in the Middle East, where authoritarian governments accompany high levels of per capita GDP. Thus, if rising incomes tend to make a government more democratic, then the exception is when rising incomes result from oil wealth, such as in Middle-Eastern countries.

Petroleum exports and exogenous rents are a considerable source of revenue and foreign exchange earnings in such countries as Saudi Arabia, United Arab Emirates, Egypt and Syria, as well as in Iraq. Estimates place Iraq's government revenue as 90 percent derived from oil while foreign exchange earnings provided from the oil sector are 80 percent (CIA, The Worldfactbook, 2012). However, while studies of oil-exporting states suggest significant petroleum revenues hinder democratization, the evidence also implies this impact varies, depending on social, political and economic factors (Crystal 1990, 209). For example, some studies of Iran's 1979 revolution theorize that oil wealth destabilized the Shah's regime by fueling rapid socioeconomic change (Skocpol 1982; Najmabadi 1987). Karl (1987) posits that oil wealth contributed to democratization in Venezuela, where oil revenue constitutes around half of government operating revenues. In general, while the evidence indicates oil impedes democracy in authoritarian states and has properties that prevent countries from moving toward pluralistic government, it does not explain what happens when a state begins as democratic. In Iraq, effective institutional engineering can protect against rentierism by creating compelling incentives that structure the behavior of political elites to encourage outcomes consistent and expectant with competitive political systems. Iraq's economic potential lies in its ability to modernize and optimize oil production. Since the liberation in 2003, oil production has roughly doubled from 1.3 million barrels per day to a 30-year high of 2.6 million barrels per day. This also represents a significant increase from Iraq's average of 2.2 million barrels a day in 2011 (CIA Worldfactbook 2012). However, it is also estimated that between 100,000 and 300,000 barrels per day of the declared oil production over the past four years could have been siphoned off through corruption or smuggling, according to a U.S. study from (Glanz 2007).

Due to improvements in the security environment, an increase in foreign investment and abundant natural resources, Iraq's GDP growth is poised for significant long-term gains. Since liberation in 2003, Iraq has seen per capita GDP grow on average by 16 percent for the last nine years. Per capita GDP for 2011 is $3,500 compared to a pre-intervention GDP of $741 in 2002 (World Bank 2012). Improving the economy and other socioeconomic conditions offers an opportunity for the new government to legitimate itself. Additionally, establishing constitutional safeguards against the exploitation of oil revenue and engineering a strong rule of law will be important to guarantee reciprocal obligations between state leaders and citizens.

We run a predictive probability analysis to compare the results of the model to actual democratic performance in Iraq (Table 5.1). We use the following assumptions in the analysis: (1) Iraq's transitional process occurred through foreign intervention; (2) Iraq adopted a parliamentary system of government; (3) its prior regime type is single-party; and (4) we are able to use Iraq's actual 2011 per capita GDP and a ten-year GDP growth rate average (2002–11) rather than relying on estimated numbers since Iraq's transitional process started in 2003.

As shown in Table 5.1, the predicted values of Iraq's transition by foreign intervention results in an average Polity score over ten years of 4.78, compared to an actual and current Polity score of 3. The model performs relatively well in this instance as little distinction exists between a Polity score of 3 and 4. While not a stable democracy at this stage, the measurement of Polity scores shows much improvement over the Hussein era score of –9.

The Arab Spring

The past half century has witnessed democratic development toward democracy around the world. Although the Middle East has lagged behind this global trend toward democracy, a number of countries have made transitions from autocracy to democracy, particularly since the Arab Spring uprising. The beginning of the Arab Spring in 2011 brought forth a hope of democratic change from dictatorship in the Middle East and introduced a new wave of democracy to the world. Through media coverage of the democratic uprisings, citizens everywhere in the world watched as the people of Tunisia, Egypt, Libya and Yemen sought to remove authoritarian regimes and install democracy. In Tunisia, Egypt and Yemen regimes were overthrown mostly peacefully, while in Libya regime change came through violence.

The recent shift towards democracy in countries around the world has provided political scientists with enough case studies to analyze the modes of transition. The shifts towards democratization in the Arab Spring are characteristic of particular modes of transition either by cooperative pact or regime collapse and have corresponding characteristics that give us insight into how these political changes are shifting towards democracy.

Table 5.1 The predicted value model of Iraq's democratic transition

Variables	Foreign intervention
Constant	4.44
Transition type	1.32
Region (North Africa and Middle East)	(0.636)
Institutional choice (parliamentary)	(0.320)
Prior regime type (single party)	(1.31)
Prior democratic history (none)	0
Per capita GDP	\$3,500* 0.000254=0.889
GDP growth rate	15.94% * 2.57=0.409
Predicted value of Polity score	**4.78**

Notes
For per capita GDP, we use the most recent data available from the World Bank, listing Iraq's 2011 per capita GDP at \$3,500. For GDP growth rate, we use a ten-year average based on World Bank statistics, which equates to 15.94 percent for the years 2002–11.

Where the predicted value equation variables are denoted by zero, this indicates that these variables were used as the baseline category in the OLS model (Table 2). Obtaining the predicted value of the Polity score is achieved through adding or subtracting the values of the variables. Parentheses around a number denote a negative number.

The understanding of the democratic transition requires extensive research. However, the research on the Arab Spring is still limited as developments are still unfolding. This study focuses on Tunisia, Egypt, Libya, and Yemen as case studies, and attempts to make best use of existing literatures and secondary sources of information in order to come up with some logical prediction for democratic prospects in these countries.

Modes of transition

Each country is a separate and unique case but contains some parallels with the modes of transition from the third wave of democratization. We will examine the key factors in the mode of transition: the main actors in the transition process and how ruling elites and opposition forces interacted to influence processes and outcomes – ruling elites from above or opposition forces from below or the combined roles of elites and opposition.

Tunisia

> Government overthrown on January 14, 2011. President Zine el Abidine Ben Ali flees into exile. Elections for a Constituent Assembly held on October 23, 2011.
>
> (National Public Radio 2011)

The starting point for regime change in Tunisia was the self-immolation of Mohamed Bouazizi in Tunisia on December 17, 2010 (Inayatullah 2011) Bouazizi, a street vendor, was repeatedly harassed by police for selling produce without a permit. When Bouazizi took his complaint to public officials he was turned away. Filled with animosity toward the political conditions, the feeling of so many Tunisians, he doused himself in a flammable liquid and set himself on fire in a crowded Tunis street. Following his suicide, mass protests throughout the country took place; by January 14, 2011 Ben Ali's regime was ousted.

Tunisia started its political transformation as a series of protests to combat the reigning authoritarian regime under Ben Ali. Youth groups took to various media outlets – airwaves, television, telephone and public non-government organizations to spread their messages and unify the public (Noueihed and Warren 2012). They called for reform and the resignation of Ben Ali. As noted by Noueihed and Warren (2012) "What had begun as localized protests in a struggling town had ended as the Jasmine Revolution, named in the Western press after the fragrant national flower that is hawked on the country's sandy beaches and in its street-side cafes" (65). The support of the Tunisian General Labor Union (UGTT) and the Tunisian National Lawyers Order for the protests played an important role in spreading the protests to a nationwide movement, and shaping its political demands (Miller 2012). When labor groups, lawyers, students, teachers, Islamic groups, rural townsfolk, residents and other social groups formed a broad cross-class coalition and joined the action for nation-wide strikes and protests, the elite was split, and the military and police force became reluctant to put down the demonstrations. When the army chief of staff refused to deploy troops in support of the police force, and even placed soldiers between the police and the protesters, Ben Ali felt hopeless and fled in exile (Nepstad 2011).

The Tunisian military is one of the smallest and poorest armies in North Africa and has members from diverse social and economic levels. It also has a tradition of being non-political, and mainly serving as a border defender. It historically had no place in the political decision making process nor took part in economic development programs. Many of the military officers received professional training in the United States and Europe where they were exposed to the principles of civil-military relations under democracy. Tunisia's military was therefore professionalized, with no political or economic interests to protect by continuing to support the Ben Ali dictatorship (Nepstad 2011). By obtaining the support of the military, protesters in Tunisia were able to push the ruler out of office (Gelvin 2012).

With the abdication of his leadership role, Ben Ali had simultaneously allowed his rule to be handed over to the leader of Parliament, pending new elections. The main actors in this political transition included those both from above and from below. Within days of Ben Ali fleeing into exile, the interim government attempted to conduct a presidential election with the goal of allowing Ben Ali's longtime Prime Minister, Mohamed Ghannouchi, to become the new president. However, protestors demanded full participation from representatives of all newly emergent parties and civil society organizations to "craft" democratic transition. With elites clamoring to change the regime after Ben Ali's departure, and the opposition demanding change, both groups are working together to craft Tunisia into a successful democracy.

The Ben Achour Commission was tasked with overseeing the process of constitutional reform and new elections. The Commission turned out to be an effective consensus-building body that worked with elites and other groups to craft electoral rules and a package of other measures to facilitate democratic transition. This laid the foundation for the October 2011 elections (Stepan 2012), which resulted in the selection of a 217-member Constitutional Assembly. An estimated 85 percent of the people went to the polls (Lust 2012).

Noueihed and Warren (2012) observe

> Yet of all the countries that saw mass uprising in 2011, Tunisia possessed more of the ingredients for a home-grown, successful revolution than any other. Its long history of political activism, which Ben Ali and his predecessor curbed but did not kill, its resilient civil society, its educated and unarmed people, its neutral army, its relative religious homogeneity and its engaged and pragmatic Islamist movement, also meant it had more of the ingredients necessary for success.

(65)

All of these elements facilitated a non-violent shift forced from the bottom yet combined with the role of elite groups from above to push out the old authoritarian regime and move toward a new democratic one.

> By the end of 2011, there was no real dispute among the main parties on the form of the future government. All the largest parties, including Ennahda, agreed on the principles of freedom of belief and expression, democracy, political pluralism and rotation of power.
>
> (Noueihed and Warren 2012, 82)

After the successful uprising, elite groups that held government influence took the demands from below and formulated a new plan. Individuals such as Ghannouchi, Béji Caïd Essebsi and Fouad Mebazaa came into power and took on interim positions, which meant that constitution drafting, law making, as well as reconstruction of the country as a whole required elites and the opposition to collaborate and prevent chaos. They agreed that the new regime should be democratic and that it should invest more in the needs of the people and take power away from those that might corrupt it. The ruling elites and the opposition worked together in negotiations to move towards a new democratic structure and create free elections and policy reforms to curtail corruption. This transplacement of power has put Tunisia on the track of democratization. Khouri (2013, 29) argues,

> In Tunisia and Egypt, citizens are directly contesting for power by forming groups that engage politically with other groups to define new state norms and policies. These include civil society organizations, religious movements, political parties, the private sector, military authorities, youth groups, labor movements, women's organizations and many others.

Cross-class coalitions are thus vital for the success of regime change, and played a key role in the countries of the Arab Spring. Where coalition groups engage in constructive opposition, revolutions would be more likely to succeed in moving towards democracy. Where they attempt to frustrate each other and create a policy paralysis, revolutions would be more likely to fail, because one group or class protest could be easily labeled by the regime as a disruptive force, and the dictator can unite elites against that threat (Goldstone 2011, 462) In Tunisia, when protestors formed a broad constructive opposition coalition, elites were split and became reluctant to support the dictator in putting down mass demonstrations. While elites from the old regime initially did not play a significant role, citizens and opposition elites from different parties, such as an-Nahda, Marzouki's party, and *at-Takattul* (The Bloc) were working together in a spirit of toleration and compromise to form a new government in the transition toward democracy (Miller *et al.* 2012, 75).

> The government dissolved the former ruling party, dismissed scores of officials close to the old regime, lifted censorship, seized the assets of more

than one hundred members of the Ben Ali-Trabelsi clan and their associates, established commissions to propose political reforms and investigate corruption and abuses under the old regime, and appointed one council to draft a new electoral law and scheduled elections for an assembly that would rewrite the constitution.

(Gelvin 2012, 63)

The creation of the new government depended solely on the cooperation and negotiation of elite leaders and citizens to draft a constitution that reflected the needs and ideals of the people. Therefore, it appears that Tunisia started from below; however, because both the elites in power as well as the opposition were at the table and there was some level of interaction that had to happen between them, we classify this transition as cooperative.

Egypt

Government overthrown on February 11, 2011. President Hosni Mubarak steps down, faces charges of killing unarmed protesters. Elections held on November 28, 2011. Protests continue in Tahrir Square.

In the case of Egypt, like that of Tunisia, the movement was sparked by those from below. Citizens of Egypt took part in protests and demonstrations to remove Mubarak from power. "Egypt's Kefaya movement demanding political reform through the middle of the decade became the regional template for wired networks of online and offline youth activists" (Lynch 2012, 13). The primary actors in Egypt are the youth of the country. Through their internet culture, their ability to mobilize quickly and effectively, and their capacity to critically challenge the authoritarian regime they emerged as the face of the movement.

However, as the movement gained traction, participants were not only youth activists, but also included labor groups, students, small business owners, professionals, Islamists and Coptic Christians, representing a broad cross-class coalition of social classes. The breadth of the coalition not only made it difficult for the dictator to find public support but also split the ruling elite and helped to persuade the army not to intervene militarily (Goldstone 2011, 459).

Mass protests among the middle and lower classes were a common occurrence in Egypt and between 1998 and 2008 protest activities increased by 400 percent (Noueihed and Warren 2012, 308) in response to rapidly deteriorating socioeconomic conditions. In the current environment, riots, strikes, demonstrations and sit-ins demanding increases in wages were undertaken by labor, civil servants and professionals in the state service sectors (Atef 2009, 12). People from all walks of Egyptian life rallied together against police brutality, corruption, state of emergency laws, censorship, inflation, high unemployment rates, increasing food prices, and low minimum wages. The demonstrations were primarily non-violent acts of resistance. They demanded the resignation and arrest of President Mubarak and his two sons for crimes against humanity. They also demanded the cancelation of State of Emergency laws, and the dissolution of Parliament and the National Democratic Party, which were instruments of patronage under Mubarak's regime (Bakry 2012). Mubarak resigned 28 days after the protests began. Two days later, the Chairman of the Supreme Council of the Armed Forces and de facto head of state, Mohamed Hussein Tantawi, announced the suspension of the constitution, dissolution of both houses of parliament, and that the military would rule until elections could be held. The end of Mubarak's rule had occurred, which signified the beginning of democracy in Egypt.

The primary actors in Egypt's political transition were those both from below and above. The protestors demanded change from the government through a broad cross-class and cross-regional coalition, and swayed the military into being a neutral party, who played a decisive role in ending the old regime. These circumstances eventually caused President Mubarak to seek exile and abdicate his leadership role. Therefore, the transition is a result of the combined roles of masses and elites.

In the transition process, powerful elite groups joined in the protests to remove Mubarak while members of his own government attempted to restrain the violence he attempted to unleash through the military. There was a cooperation compromising social organizations, established opposition parties, and politicians that joined the uprising soon after it broke out (Gelvin 2012, 52). That is, they mobilized from below and used compromise and negotiation tactics with elites to make non-violent demands for regime change and eventually transform to popular direct action, sometimes violent, to force the old regime to shift. "In Egypt alone, the last few years of the 2000s saw thousands of labor strikes as well as protests by pillars of society such as judges and lawyers" (Lynch 2012, 13), which highlights the connection between the mobilizing masses and certain elite groups that joined together to protest against the authoritarian regime.

The military elites were a key actor that also played a decisive role in the transition process. The military had shifted from a dominant role to one of a subordinate role to the civilian government under Mubarak's rule. Its subsequent professionalism increased significantly, with its main role carrying out defense and foreign policies rather than influencing domestic politics. The withdrawal of the military from domestic politics ensured civilian control over the government and transformed the military into an interest group with its institutional interests that competed with other institutional and societal interest groups. The military also played an economic role that was involved in the production of military hardware and household goods, defense industries, national infrastructure and agriculture, which provided the Egyptian military with financial and institutional independence (Harb 2003).

In the widespread protests, military elites were also concerned about the dynastic ambitions of Mubarak who was grooming his son to take over from him (Goldstone 2011). Military elites and officers were afraid that if Mubarak's son took over, they could lose economically. The Egyptian military had amassed valuable real estate holdings and industrial investments that would have been jeopardized under his son's proposed policies (Nepstad 2011, 489). Soldiers on the front line also refused to fire at the protesters and then the military made public its position by stating that it would not use force to stop the protests. Continuing mass protests through a broad cross-class coalition and the lack of support from the military created the final straw and Mubarak resigned.

Unlike Tunisia, however, the military remained in power after the overthrow of the authoritarian regime. With this type of structure in place the type of transformation of the regime is best classified as cooperative, suggesting negotiations between opposition and incumbents facilitated the transition. As Gelvin (2012, 64) argues,

> Egypt's military acted swiftly to meet some of the high-profile demands of the protest movement … they forced out Mubarak's prime minister, dissolved the NDP and one of the leading security forces, appointed a commission to oversee amending the constitution, and, once the commission had done its work, organized a referendum on the amendments as the first step toward parliamentary elections.

Unfortunately, the road to democracy is jeopardized, to a certain degree, by allowing the military to remain in control of the government. Galvin (2012, 64) suggests,

> The military much preferred stability to reform. Egypt's rulers dragged their feet on some of the uprising's central demands and took a confrontational stance towards workers who continued their strike wave as well as protesters who continued their demonstrations. And far from democrats in uniform, the military continued to use torture against those who 'disturbed the peace', forced women to undergo "virginity tests" while detained, and, in an obvious warning to others, sentenced a blogger to prison for three years for criticizing the military.

While certain reforms have been implemented, the country still has a long way to go and massive changes in government must occur to create a stable and effective democracy. The power still, obviously, stands with the elites with some negotiation occurring with the opposition. The opposition is struggling to negotiate with those in power to shift the government towards democracy and address the needs and wants of the people. The events of the Arab Spring have brought change. As was the case before the mass demonstrations and protests, elections were also utilized as a method to secure access to state resources. Furthermore, elections have failed to rally all those who occupied the streets leading to a highly polarized situation in Egypt (DuPont and Passey 2011).

Libya

> Anti-government protests begin on February 15, 2011, leading to civil war between opposition forces and Moammar Gadhafi loyalist. Tripoli was

captured and the government overthrown on August 23, 2011. Gadhafi was killed by Transition forces on October 20, 2011, and free and peaceful multiparty elections were held in July 2012.

Libya began its revolution and demand for shift towards democracy in January and February of 2011. As noted by Goldstone (2011, 459)

> As in Tunisia, the Libyan Revolution began with local protests mainly by one group – in this case lawyers. However, the movement gradually spread to form a cross-regional and cross-class coalition, with help from NATO, to overcome Colonel Gadhafi's mercenary and praetorian guard forces.

Cross-class coalitions were important factors in the overthrow of the government just as they were in Tunisia and Egypt. Inspired by the Tunisian and Egyptian transitions, lawyers began the protests in Libya, hoping to inspire a peaceful movement, but were met with resistance and imprisoned by Qaddafi's police forces. Then, more lawyers joined in and assembled in front of the police headquarters in support of a human rights lawyer who had been arrested. They too were broken up by a brutal crackdown, which led to even further protests and the setting fire to police vehicles and government buildings. A National Conference for the Libyan Opposition was formed and called for all social groups to take action to oppose the Qaddafi regime. Thus, lawyers were joined by students, teachers, professionals, workers and Islamists, spreading to form a broad cross-class and cross-regional coalition to overthrow Qaddafi's regime (Goldstone 2011, 462). Soon thereafter, the elites became fragmented with some government officials and officers joining ranks with the rebel forces (Gelvin 2012, 81) The fact that elites defected from the government and joined the rebel forces was crucial in overcoming Qaddafi's forces.

The elite defecting and supporting the challenging coalition or refusing to cooperate in violent suppression were critical factors in shaping transition outcomes. When dictators in Tunisia and Egypt realized that they could not count on the military to suppress the uprisings, they choose to flee into exile. Alternatively, Qaddafi, who felt that he could depend on the personal loyalty of his military, was then determined to crush the uprising. When he failed to do so, his regime crumbled and was replaced by rebel forces (Alimi and Meyer 2012, 477).

Tribes played an important role in the overthrow of Qaddafi's regime. The tribe is one of the strongest social organizations in Libya and still a major source of personal identification in Libyan society. Some of the tribes were anti-Qaddafi, some were pro-Qaddafi, and some unclear. Western tribes formed the core of support for Qaddafi's regime over the decades, while periodic rebellions against his rule originated among eastern tribes centered on the city of Benghazi.

The military in Libya was divided and made up of several parts, some of which were professionals, some were mercenaries who were employed to protect Qaddafi, and some other units were made up of tribal groups loyal to the Qaddafi family. Most of the professionals in the army actively joined with the opposition or refused to be deployed against the opposition (Goldstone 2012, 459). It was important that some in the military were hesitant to intervene to stop the protests and allowed the protests to continue. Qaddafi had no safe way to exit because he was dependent on the personal loyalty of certain members of the military (Brynen *et al.*, 2012, 20) Many in or close to Libya's National Transitional Council – the anti-Qaddafi government established early on in the uprising – were former government officials or military officers in the Qaddafi regime (Goodwin 2011, 454).

Rebel groups, through a cross-class and cross-regional coalition, partnered with NATO to bring to an end Qaddhafi's reign. By the end of August 2011, rebels had forcibly and violently overthrown all of Qaddhafi's strongholds and military presence in every town and city as well as his own compound. Outside influences, both within the region and internationally, played a role in assisting those primary actors in overthrowing the authoritarian regime. Thus, the mode of transition in Libya is typically a replacement (collapse) of Qaddafi's regime. Transition occurred through overthrow of the existing regime by rebel groups with limited, if any, help from incumbent elites.

"In a stunning turn of events, the first post-Qaddafi election produced a landslide victory for a wide-ranging coalition of moderate, liberal and secular parties" (Ghitis 2012). The winner of the election was the National Forces Alliance (NFA), made up of smaller parties and organizations headed by Mahmoud Jibril, who took as many votes as all other parties combined and more than double those of its main rival, the Muslim Brotherhood's Justice and Construction Party (JCP), which was widely expected to win. Non-Islamist parties won because they formed a cohesive and broad coalition and rejected the Brotherhood's strategy to side with Islamist parties. "Instead, the NFA has a strong nationalist identity that incorporates Libya's Muslim character. By current Arab standards, that counts as secular" (Ghitis 2012). Ordinary people preferred peace and stability after civil war to possible armed conflicts or protests led by an extremist Islamic party.

Just as issues in Egypt and Tunisia popped up after the overthrow of the authoritarian governments, Libya grappled with its own set of issues. While different social classes had band together to overthrow the likes of Qaddafi, Mubarak and Ali they soon would fall apart in the race for power.

> Yet while alliances work well with a simple goal, once that goal is achieved the cross-class coalitions in revolutions and revolts frequently start to fracture. With the main goal of eliminating the old leader completed, the reverse groups in the coalition quickly return to pursuing their own goals.
>
> (Goldstone 2011, 460)

Elitist groups and ordinary protesters who once shared the same political agenda during the uprising are now against each other as they compete for power and the opportunity to shape the new political landscape. With democracy on the horizon, but still in a fragile state, it is a challenge for all parties or groups from above and those from below to create a stable democratic government.

The formation of the new government was a transformation process that emerged from the regime collapse. The opposition was the most significant and dominant role in creating a new government in Libya. "The rebels had to establish a government so that they might maintain order, organize rudimentary services and defense, gain international support, claim Qaddafi's overseas assets, and sell the national patrimony, oil" (Gelvin 2012, 85). The opposition completely replaced the old regime in order to carry out reforms they felt the liberalized parts of the country needed. They quickly adopted an agenda to meet those needs. "The council included the heads of local councils established in liberated towns" (85). While the establishment of the new government took place, its stability still remains to be seen.

Yemen

> Ongoing protests since February 3, 2011. President Ali Abdullah Saleh is injured in an attack on June 4, 2011. On November 23, 2001, he signs a power transfer agreement ending his 33-year reign. On February 21, 2012, a presidential election that formally ousted Saleh begins a new era in Yemen. Al-Hadi takes office for a two-year term before new parliamentary and presidential elections in 2014.

In the case of Yemen, initially the protests were made up of elitist leaders of different opposition parties who were opposing parliament's plan to abolish term limits. After the government diffused the movement and made concessions, the movement's primary actors shifted to students (particularly those at university) and workers. Eventually they were joined by influential tribe leaders (elites) that were the backbone of the authoritarian regime's stability.

> The regime in Yemen depended on the compliance, or at least the quiescence, of the influential tribal, political, and military leaders whom it bought and balanced off against one another. As the protest movement broadened its base of support and spread throughout the country, provoked further resistance, those leaders smelled blood in the water and began to defect.
>
> (Gelvin 2012, 80)

The military in Yemen became divided when protesters were brutally killed by the police force, and when General Ali Mohsen al-Ahmar defected, and a dozen generals joined him (Barany 2011, 29).

The elite interaction with the opposition became one of unity. They helped each other to create mass mobilization against Saleh and overthrow the regime. The division among the elite also played an important role in fostering the protests. Saleh relied on his relatives in the military and security forces to maintain control, but when the protesters increased their support among the people and the violence against them created further resistance, some of the political and military leaders began to change sides. Armed combat took place between Hasid tribesmen and the military who had joined the protesters against government security forces and military who remained loyal to Saleh (Gelvin 2012, 80) The Gulf Cooperation Council (GCC) attempted to negotiate an end to the crisis peacefully, but Saleh refused to accept and sign the agreement. More military units joined the opposition fighting against Saleh's loyalist armed forces, and some protest groups, Islamic militants, tribal group fighters, and military units occupied government buildings and streets in some major cities, and the conflict intensified. Although Saleh indicated he would sign the plan, he changed his mind and refused to do so three times. An assassination attempt left him injured and he left the country for Saudi Arabia.

> The defection of the prominent army general, Ali Muhsin Al-Ahmar, a member of the president's tribe, gave Yemen's revolution an extraordinary push. Equally important was the defection of tribal leaders in the areas of Marib, Khawlan, Sa'ada, Shabwa, among them even sheikhs from the president's Al-Ahmar clan who joined the revolution against Ali Saleh.[2]

In September 2011, Saleh returned to Yemen and by November, due to increasing pressure by the people and key elite groups, such as the military (Ali Muhsin), the tribe (the al-Ahmars) and Islamism (Abdulmajid al-Zindani), Saleh eventually accepted a GCC plan that allowed him to resign in exchange for immunity from prosecution, and agreed to transfer power to his vice-president, Abd Rabbuh Mansur Hadi. A presidential election was subsequently held in February of 2012 in which Hadi was elected. He was the sole candidate on the ballot, and the absence of other candidates was the result of fractured opposition forces. With the election of Hadi, the 33-year rule of Saleh was effectively ended and the second phase of the GCC plan was ushered in that puts forth a comprehensive national dialogue, the amendment of the constitution, and new elections with two years.

Yemen's path shifting toward a democratic political system was much bumpier that of Tunisia and Egypt and did not bring about immediate democratic results (Schumacher 2012, 132). With the help of international powers, that of Saudi Arabia and the United States, Saleh finally accepted a compromise written by the Gulf Cooperation Council that would allow Saleh to resign and gain immunity if a national unity government could run the country until elections could be held (Gelvin 2012, 86). With the election of a new president, Yemen faces a series of large obstacles in its possible shift towards democracy. The transition in Yemen is complex. The violent nature of the process suggests an incumbent regime resistant to change and therefore contains features of regime collapse. On the other hand, however, numerous tribal elites and military defections from the regime suggest a process shaped to some degree by cooperative mode, in addition to the sitting vice-president assuming the presidency until the 2014 election. Because of this, we tentatively argue that Yemen is a cooperative transition, a result of joint forces of elites in power and in opposition. Tribal groups and opposition remain against the old regime practices that are still in place under the new regime. While the new regime faces uncertainty from their new president and being the hotspot for Al-Qaeda movement and occupation, the plan to create a democracy has not been made clear (DuPont and Passey 2012). "The protectors are frustrated that their movement has been co-opted by elites who play according to the same old highly personalized 'rules of the game' outside of Yemen's weak formal institutions" (Thiel 2012). How to balance between inclusiveness and efficiency, between the old and new regime, stability and democracy, ultimately how to create an inclusive, democratic rule with which all parties agree, is an enormous challenge in the transitional period before the 2014 election. Based on the analysis against the literature on the modes of transition, Libya is typical of a regime *collapse* while Tunisia, Egypt and Yemen can be categorized as *cooperative*.

Causes of transition

Bouazizi's self-immolation was the single spark that provoked the Arab Spring, but the conditions across these countries had made it possible for such sparks to create contagion at that time (Alimi and Meyer 2012, 476). What factors constituted the conditions of the Arab Spring that brought about the end of long-standing autocracy and created the hope of democratic transition in these countries? Many scholars, including Huntington, believe that Middle Eastern culture is not synonymous with democracy because the overwhelming majority of the region is Muslim. Clearly Huntington's analysis has been challenged by the Arab Spring. These countries have made it clear they yearn for democracy, which is applicable to all cultures. Even prior to the Arab Spring, Kamrava (2007) disputed what most scholars suggested and believed that the Third Wave would reach the Middle East.

Economic development is considered a key indicator in creating democracy. Kamrava (2007) argues, "developing countries feature processes of economic development that are inimical to democratic openings" (197). Tunisia, Egypt, Libya, and Yemen all demonstrated that they met the basic conditions for democratization in many areas as typified in modernization theory. Although unemployment and poverty were widespread, they had a growing middle class, civil society, educated population, and widespread use of social media as a result of modernization.

The following section will look into the causes of democratization by examining key indicators derived from different theoretical approaches to democratic transitions. According to Pridham and Vanhanen (1994), "Theoretical approaches to democratic transition have not presented any coherent or even elaborate body of work" (2). Transition theory has in fact tended to "diverge" between different schools of thought. Przeworski points out that studies on democratic transition can be loosely grouped into two categories: studies that focus on the objective conditions of regime transformation and studies that concentrate on political strategies and choices (Przeworski 1991). These approaches are discussed in Chapter 2.

The rich literature has generated at least four main theoretical approaches that can be employed to identify causal factors that explain democratic transition, including (1) structuralist approach; (2) process-driven approach; (3) institutionalist approach; and (4) political economy approach.

Modernization theories are a structuralist approach that focuses on the changes of social and economic structure as a result of modernization that prepare a set of macro-level social and economic conditions for democratic transition, such as socioeconomic development, political culture, rising middle class and independent civil society.

The *process-driven* approach, on the other hand, focuses on the political process in which elites in power or in opposition, or both, interact with one another to make strategic choices for democratic change. The process-driven approach also explores how elites play an important role in ending the old regime and bringing about democratic change.

The *institutionalist approach* emphasizes the impact of institutions on the formation of policies and patterns of political actions that may act in favor of or against political or social movement, and also stresses the role of institutions in shaping and constraining the objectives and preferences of political actors. How the regime is institutionalized is seen as the explanatory variable for the variations in regime transition (March and Olsen 1984; Evans *et al.* 1985; Krasner 1988; Powell and DiMaggio 1991; Steinmo *et al.* 1992; O'Neil 1996). Institutional scholars focus on the links between elite strategic choice and the "confined contexts" that determine the very parameters of political action. They attempt to bridge the links between structures, institutions and elite contingent choice by pointing out the limits of the ... approaches (Karl 1990).

Political economy approach emphasizes the effect of short-term economic conditions or the impact of economic crises on the terms of transition and nature of political alignments (Haggard and Kaufman 1997). The loss of legitimacy in the eyes of the public as a result of economic crisis often leads to a regime transition, and deteriorating economic performance cuts across all social strata and is often the impetus for change. The power and legitimacy of a regime is compromised when fiscal mismanagement and irresponsibility leads to economic crises. One of the underlying assumptions is the correlation between economic crisis and regime change. Failure to conquer economic crisis and manage the resulting distributive conflicts would increase the probability of the old regime being transformed Similarly, successful adjustment to economic crisis and improvement of economic performance would increase the prospects for democratic consolidation, and *vice versa* (Haggard and Kaufman 1995). Scholars like Haggard and Kaufman (1997) posited that economic crises reduces the power and legitimacy of authoritarian incumbents and enfranchises the opposition's bargaining power to prompt a democratic transition. They measure economic performance by declining growth, and accelerating inflation, which adversely affects a wide array of social groups. They assert the weaknesses of strategic interaction theory in quantifying the external conditions which force political elites into action. Their theory draws on strategic analysis but focuses on the effects of economic conditions on the preferences, resources and strategies of key political actors in the transition "game." They concede that poor economic performance is neither sufficient nor necessary to bring about authoritarian withdrawal, but disrupts the political bargains rulers forge with the public sector (Haggard and Kaufman 1997). Mounting discontent due to unsavory economic conditions can unite the public and rally them into action to strip ineffective and illegitimate authoritarian regimes of their power.

Haggard and Kaufman focus on the strategic actions of three important social groups who bring about regime transitions. First affected are private sector business groups, who initially focus on changes in economic policy or government personnel (Haggard and Kaufman 1997, 267). The inability of the government to react quickly and effectively results in defection of this group, which greatly diminishes the ruler's authority. Another group affected by economic crises is the middle and lower income groups, who are historically vulnerable to political repression. Mounting discontent amongst this group results in mass mobilization of strikes, protests and street demonstrations that disrupt the social order. Their motives are often apolitical and are generally a reactionary response to unemployment, inflation, and declining real wages. The most crucial to the survival of authoritarian regimes is the continuing loyalty of the military elite. The proximate cause for the exit of authoritarian regimes can almost always be found in a split within the ruling elite (Haggard and Kaufman 1997, 271). The deteriorating economic conditions provide these groups with the necessary ammunition to dethrone ineffective authoritarian regimes and replace them with democratic ones.

All these approaches have some basic empirical indicators for the causes of democratization. Although the underlying causes of the Arab Spring are similar to the Third Wave, some of the causes were political crimes and offenses, financial crises and unemployment (Joffé 2011) Springborg (2011) also argues that unemployment and the financial crises in Tunisia, Egypt and Libya were the precursor to regime transitions. Therefore, it appears the political economy approach is a better fit in explaining transition. This study attempts to examine these factors to offer some tentative explanations for the causes of the uprising in the countries under study.

Tunisia

Deteriorating Economic conditions: Tunisia experienced sustained economic growth of more than 5 percent since the mid-1990s, resulting in sharp increases in trade with the EU, foreign direct investment, tourism, living standards, middle class, educated population, and health care (El-Khawas 2012, 7). Therefore, Tunisia had good economic performance compared to other countries in the region over the past decade in terms of both GDP per capita and the annual growth rate. However, in 2008 Tunisia began an economic downturn due to the global financial crisis and sharp drop in trading with European countries. The country had a high unemployment rate among educated youth, which became the catalyst of the protest movement. The official statistics show 19 percent unemployment rate among this segment of the population in 2007, but unofficial statistics suggest figures are twice as high as those published by the government (Paciello 2011). Some studies confirm the grave picture of high unemployment at the time of public uprising that brought down the regime, and suggest a 30 percent unemployment rate among college educated graduates. Mohammed al-Bouazizi, the fruit vendor who set himself on fire in protest in front of a government building, was a college graduate. Educated youth were unable to gain employment and became discontented with the ruler, and they acted together to bring change to end the old regime (Borgan 2010).

Regional disparity in living conditions between coastal cities and interior regions was another major problem and challenge that led to demonstrations in the years leading up to the 2010 widespread unrest that brought down the regime. While coastal cities benefited from tourism and foreign investment and had good economic performance, the economy in the interior regions stagnated, with living conditions deteriorating and the unemployment rate ranging from 25 to 40 percent. The people of the interior regions believed they did not receive their fair share of public investment that fueled economic growth in coastal cities. However, the government was unable to create new jobs and improve the regional balance of living standards, and thus lost legitimacy with most of the Tunisian people (Paciello 2011).

In late 2010, the WikiLeaks release of secret cables, spreading over Facebook, Twitter, blogger, etc., exposed the corruption of Ben Ali's family and his inner circle, and increased popular discontent at the time of economic downturn and high unemployment, particularly among the youth who account for 40 percent of population. Although the government promised to boost employment by offering a new $10 million employment program, it was too late, as protesters did not trust the government's promises. When another youth subsequently killed himself in the midst of demonstration, the local protest spread quickly cross the country (El Khawas 2012, 9).

Social media are one of the significant results of modernization, and also played an important role in the protests in Tunisia. Social media did not make the revolution but rather facilitated it. People made the revolution in the context of their times, which is the one of information and new communication technology that has been brought about by modernization. Revolutions in the past were not mobilized through social media, which has increased both the scope and speed of change. Facebook™, Twitter™, and other social media today, interacting with other factors, helped to spread the word and magnitude of protests quickly as they were used by various groups in encouraging ordinary citizens to take to the streets (Haerens and Zott 2013). Tunisian people watched videos on YouTube™ about the abusive police and could access foreign news coverage of political corruption online. Individuals and groups also used digital media to arrive at strategies for action and collective goals. The government tried to ban social media outlets, but, hackers outside the country provided new software to help protesters and social groups get around the state firewalls and online censorship (Howard and Hussain 2011).

Most importantly, it changed traditional ways of communication in mobilizing opposition groups. The result of social media is a new mode of communication and coordination (Diani 2011), and the spread of modernity, freedom and democracy. Social media has helped unite a broad cross-class and cross-regional coalition that are potent enough to thwart an authoritarian regime's effort to target one group or segment of society through mass mobilization. Amateur video and narratives of eyewitness accounts uploaded to blogs and sites became a major source for news coverage as events were unfolding. "Tunisian activists were able to use social media to document the scope of unrest—and the police's brutal response to it" (Miller *et al.* 2012, 71).

Modernization and globalization have brought about new ways of communication and coordination in mobilization. The result is the ability to provide information to the citizenry that the regime might otherwise try to block. The growing middle class and civil society organizations are effectively utilizing social media and technology to educate people and organize collective actions to effect regime change.

In order to make democracy work, the new Tunisian government needs to focus on reducing unemployment and fixing the economy. The new government has reached out to the United States; it discussed an aid package in late 2011, and the Peace Corps will go to Tunisia to help with youth development programs. Tunisia's prospects appear to be the most optimistic of the Arab Spring transitions due to the role of its professional, non-political military. Tunisia has perhaps the best chance of effecting real democratic change because its transition to a democracy is protected by a professional but non-political military. Even here, the question remains as to what role Islam and Islamists will play in the political environment of the new Tunisia. However, many scholars of modernization theory consider Tunisia as having the most promising social and economic "preconditions" for democracy as it has a relatively developed economy, a better educated population and a fairly moderate Islam (Plattner 2011). According to Bruce Maddy-Weitzman's (2011) profile of Huntington's (1991,11) *Third Wave*,

> there was no Arab state on his list, yet he identified Tunisia as a prime candidate for future democratization owing to its pace of economic growth, educated middle class, and concurrent liberalization measures undertaken by the country's new president, Ben Ali.

Tunisia was the only Arab state on the radar for democracy as early as 1991. The following predictive model tests the probability of democratic prospects in Tunisia.

Under the predicted value simulation of Tunisia's democratic transition, we can determine Polity scores (the dependent variable) for Tunisia at any of the intervals listed in Table 5.2. We use model 4 (the ten-year Polity average) as substantively it is the most meaningful. Through a predicted value equation, we determine Tunisia's average Polity rating ten years after a hypothetical

Table 5.2 The predicted value model of Tunisia's democratic transition

Variables	Cooperative transition
Constant	4.44
Transition type	2.91
Region (North Africa & Middle East)	(0.636)
Institutional choice (presidential)	0
Prior regime type (single party)	(1.31)
Prior democratic history (none)	0
Per capita GDP	$4,297* 0.000254 = 1.09
GDP growth rate	6.66% * 2.57 = 0.171
Predicted value of Polity score	**6.67**

Notes

For per capita GDP, we use the most recent data available from the CIA Worldfactbook, listing Tunisia's 2011 per capita GDP at $4,297. For GDP growth rate, we use a ten-year average based on historical statistics, which equate to 6.66 percent for the years 2001–10.

Where the predicted value equation variables are denoted by zero, this indicates that these variables were used as the baseline category in the OLS model (Table 2). Obtaining the predicted value of the Polity score is achieved through adding or subtracting the values of the variables. Parentheses around a number denote a negative number.

democratic transition. We use the following assumptions: (1) Tunisia transitioned through cooperative pact; (2) it has adopted a presidential system of government; (3) its prior regime type is single party; and (4) We use Tunisia's 2011 per capita GDP and a ten-year GDP growth rate average (2001–10).

The predicted values of Table 5.2 shows that Tunisia's transition by cooperative pact results in an average Polity score over ten years of 6.67, assuming a presidential system of government, an average growth rate of 6.66 percent and per capita GDP of $4,297. A Polity score of 6.67 constitutes a vast improvement over the pre-transition Polity IV score of –4.

Egypt

Deteriorating Economic conditions: Egypt has faced various sociopolitical problems: poor institutional performance, political corruption, poverty and high unemployment. Protests in Egypt started on January 25 and were largely fueled by the news from Tunisia, which then spread to Libya and other countries.

Economic conditions had improved for the last decade in terms of both GDP per capita and growth rates under Mubarak. However, recent deteriorating economic conditions, high unemployment, police abuses, government corruption, and the suppression of freedoms and civil rights that were present in Tunisia were also present in Egypt as expressed in a popular slogan at the time "bread, freedom, social justice" (Miller, 85). Prior to regime change, Egypt was suffering from inflation as well as record high unemployment coupled with rising food and fuel prices. This created inflationary pressures toward the end of 2010.[3]

According to the Economist Intelligence Unit, Egypt's average recorded unemployment for 2011 was a record high 12.2 percent. At least 90 percent of the unemployed are less than 30 years old and many more are affected by underemployment.[4] The educated youth are frustrated about their worsening situation. Out of frustration they took to the streets to protest against unemployment and the government. The unemployment rate would be much higher if those who left the workforce and are no longer seeking work are included in statistics. In Egypt, 60 percent of males aged 18 to 29 are no longer looking for work while 83 percent of women in that age group are also kept out of the workforce because no jobs are available (Gelvin 2012, 20). In a survey of public opinion in Egypt in April, 2011, 64 percent of those polled indicated that the main reason for their participation in the protests and overthrow of the government was the low standard of living and/or the high unemployment rate (Schlumberger *et al.* 2012, 107). In the midst of global economic crisis, the government had difficulty coping with the challenges of people who suffered from food crisis, inflation and unemployment. In order to deal with the challenges, the government became aggressive in imposing emergency law, which created public anger and widespread protests against the Mubarak regime that culminated in calling for his resignation. This seems to confirm the political economic approach that says that the greater the economic crisis, the greater the chance of democratic uprising.

Disparities of wealth and corruption: There were huge disparities of wealth in the Mubarak era. A large proportion of the Egyptian population is poor. According to the United Nations Development Programme (UNDP 2010), at least 20 percent of Egyptian citizens lived below the poverty level, while 14 percent of children did not attend school. For the past 20 years, poor families have been unable to provide their children's basic needs such as food, clothing, health, education and shelter. At the opposite end is a small proportion of people that hold exorbitant amounts of wealth. Economic disparity and outright corruption led to public anger and frustration among the Egyptian people (Hamdy 2011). Corruption in the Mubarak regime was extremely high:

> the litany of complaints against Mubarak is well-known to anyone who has spent time in Egypt: the police are brutal, elections are rigged, corruption is rampant, life gets more difficult for the masses, as the rich grow richer and the poor grow poorer.[5]

Social media: As in Tunisia, the Egyptian protests involved extensive use of social media, which led to spontaneous gatherings that promoted secular and non-violent protests. Egypt has the region's second largest Internet-using population, and almost everyone has access to a cell phone. The news about the departure of Ben Ali spread rapidly over Facebook, Twitter and smart message service (SMS). The government-run media gave the exile of Ben Ali grudging coverage while slowly reporting on the protests in neighboring states. The people's voice on social media was effectively linked with overseas networks of all kinds, providing streaming to cell phones and Internet media, while the government was unable to shut them down (Howard and Hussain 2011, 38).

The initial call for demonstrations in Cairo's Liberation Square on January 25, 2011 was put out via Facebook, and the most significant of these groups were the "April 6th Movement," "We Are All Khalid Sa'id," and "Youth for Justice and Freedom." They all had a youth base, and the April 6th Movement was aligned with the labor movement, with large followers on Facebook. Students and labor leaders using the Internet called for protests and in several of Egypt's cities thousands of protestors came out (Miller 2012, 93).

> They found solidarity through digital media, and then used their mobile phones to call their social networks into the streets. Protests scaled up quickly, leaving regime officials and outside observers alike surprised that such a large network of relatively liberal, peaceful, middle class citizens would mobilize against Mubarak with such speed.
>
> (Howard and Hussain 2011, 38–39)

Another well known example was the creation of the "Facebook Freedom Fighter," Wael Ghonim's, Facebook page. The page, created after seeing a photograph of Khaled Said beaten to death by police in Alexandria, became a hub for activists. It drew hundreds of thousands of members within the first day, and sparked some of the largest protests and demonstrations in Tahrir Square (Ghonim 2012). Even before the protests began, satellite television, Internet and social sites allowed for the spread of modern ideas to this newly emerging, highly literate generation. Satellite television, through its constant streaming abilities, has enabled the viewing and interpretation of western culture, complete with its highs and lows, to an eager new audience within the Arab world. The new ideas made available through globalized technology gave the Arab community much more to aspire to than a constant cycle of poverty. It made them irritated with censorship and the restrictions they face each day. Most importantly, it led them to begin to challenge laws and practices that limited their personal freedoms.

Many explained the Arab Spring as the result of deteriorating economic conditions, unemployment, disparities of wealth and corruption, but social media made important casual contributions to the success of regime change. Social media facilitated the spread of modernity, freedom, and democracy across all social classes and groups. It helped people realize the root causes of the problems under Mubarak and other dictators. It also served as an outlet to share grievances, inspire actions, and build a social movement network. The role of digital media in social movement that brought down the old regime has been consistent across the region (Howard and Hussain 2011).

In looking at prospects for democracy, the Egyptian military may serve as a facilitator or preventer to a smooth transition to democracy, as many elements of the society previously united in their opposition to Murbarak are now fighting among themselves, particularly with the influence of the Muslim Brotherhood and more radical Salafist groups. Egypt's prospects and likelihood of democratic consolidation appear to be dependent, to a large degree, on the role of the military in the transition process as it was heavily involved in all aspects of the society and the economy. Moreover, Egypt is poorer and more populous than Tunisia, and will face greater challenges in democratic transition and consolidation. Better economic performance and social policies could help to bring out brighter prospects for democracy in Egypt.

Running a predicted value simulation of Egypt's potential move towards democracy, we again use model 4 of the ten-year Polity average. Through the predicted value analysis we determine Egypt's average Polity rating ten years after transition using the following assumptions: (1) Egypt transitioned through cooperative mode; (2) It has adopted a presidential system of government; (3) Its prior regime type is personalistic; and (4) We use Egypt's 2011 per capita GDP and a ten-year GDP growth rate average (2001–10).

The predicted values of Egypt's transition by regime collapse results in an average Polity score over ten years of 7.0, assuming a presidential system of government, an average growth rate of 6.93 percent and per capita GDP of $2,781.

Libya

Libya is an oil rich country, deriving 58 percent of GDP by oil revenue. Libya is an "upper middle income" country with GDP per capita, human development index, and literacy rates all higher than Tunisia and Egypt.[6] However, Libya's corruption perception index in 2010 was 2.2, ranking 146th out of 178 countries, worse than that of Egypt (ranked 98th) and Tunisia (ranked 59th).[7] Qaddafi

Table 5.3 The predicted value model of Egypt's democratic transition

Variables	Cooperative transition
Constant	4.44
Transition type	2.91
Region (North Africa and Middle East)	(0.636)
Institutional choice (Pres)	0
Prior regime type (personalistic)	(0.598)
Prior democratic history (none)	0
Per capita GDP	$2,781* 0.000254=0.706
GDP growth rate	6.93% * 2.57=0.178
Predicted value of Polity score	**7.00**

Notes
For per capita GDP, we use the most recent data available from the CIA Worldfactbook, listing Egypt's 2011 per capita GDP at $2,781. For GDP growth rate, we use a ten-year average based on historical statistics, which equates to 6.93 percent for the years 2001–10.

Where the predicted value equation variables are denoted by zero, this indicates that these variables were used as the baseline category in the OLS model (Table 2). Obtaining the predicted value of the Polity score is achieved through adding or subtracting the values of the variables. Parentheses around a number denote a negative number.

siphoned off the country's wealth (mainly generated by oil and gas) and public funds for personal and family interest and business. He had accumulated and hidden multi-billion dollars of assets in foreign countries. "The main vehicle for the Gaddhafi's wealth is the $70 billion Libyan Investment Authority (LIA), a 'sovereign wealth fund' set up in 2006 to spend the country's oil money."[8] Corruption was widespread among government officials, military and security officers who also used public funds and commercial contracts for personal enhancement, including contracts with the international companies operating in the Libyan market. "The protests in 2011 that led to the fall of Qaddafi were in part fuelled by rampant corruption inherent in the system."[9] The Libyan people's discontent with the corrupt Qaddafi government is one of the major causes that prompted mass demonstrations following the uprisings in Tunisia and Egypt.

Deteriorating economic conditions were also important in causing the protests that occurred in Libya. The main causes for Libya's transition were hiking unemployment rates and unequal distribution of wealth between different tribal groups. Unemployment was high, estimated at over one-third of population, especially among the educated youth, estimated at 50 percent of the youth, as a result of global economic recession and international sanctions in 2011 (Gelvin 2012, 70). The government was unable to create jobs and provide economic improvements for the population. The Jasmine Revolution in the Arab world inspired the Libyan people to take action and brought disparate people together against Qaddafi's regime.

Injustice in tribal distribution of power and resources under Qaddafi was another cause of the uprising against his rule which created the East-West divide. Unlike Tunisia and Egypt, Libya is made up of tribes and clans. However, under Qaddafi's rule, some tribes, including his own and other allied tribes in the west, were privileged and received employment and advancement in security force and government sectors, while the east was discriminated against and marginalized in material gain and government sectors (Vira *et al.* 2011, 66). People and tribes in the east had resented the patronage and privilege of Qaddafi's tribes, and they were inspired by the uprising in its neighboring country, Egypt, and began to revolt against Qaddafi.

Social media also played an important role in the upheaval in Libya though Qaddafi had tight control over the Internet. The official media only reported pro-Qaddafi protests and portrayed anti-Qaddafi protests as foreign plots. Anti-Qaddafi's forces, social movement activists and various social groups had to use social media. They even used dating websites to get around the government website monitor and pass secret messages to other revolutionaries. As the *New York Times* reported, one of the most popular sites for the protesters was libyaFeb17.com, which congregates Twitter posts and helped to galvanize Qaddafi's scattered opponents abroad in English and Arabic. Protesters have posted videos to the site, filmed on mobile phones, showing the violent crackdown in several Libyan towns (MeKay 2011).

Since the fall of Qaddafi, Libya has seen a flourishing of new media outlets and free expression. Libya has good prospects for democracy because the Libyan people are eager for peace and stability, and the country has an advantage – small population and rich oil resources. Libya has the resources for economic recovery and growth. According to the *Africa Research Bulletin* (2012), it contains Africa's biggest oil reserves of over 40 billion barrels, over $100 billion in foreign reserves, and a further $150 billion in its sovereign fund. The country also has a higher literacy rate than its neighbors. Many members of the new government received Western education and maintained contacts with western countries, which might be an advantage for Libyan economic growth. Unlike Egypt, Libya does not have much religious diversity. The vast majority of the population are Sunni Muslims, leaving little scope for the kind of sectarian violence that followed Mubarak's downfall (Ghosh *et al.* 2011). The following tests the probability of democratic prospects in Libya.

Libya's potential move towards democracy, and predicted value analysis operates under the following assumptions: (1) Libya transitioned through regime collapse; (2) It adopts a presidential system of government; (3) Its prior regime type is personalistic; and (4) We use Libya's 2011 per capita GDP and a nine-year GDP growth rate average (2002–10). The predicted values of Libya's transition by regime collapse results in an average Polity score over ten years of 5.94, assuming a presidential system of government, an average growth rate of 10.74 percent and per capita GDP of $5,691.

Yemen

The 2011 Yemeni revolution occurred in a time of economic difficulty though it is rich in oil and gas resources. The uprising was in response to high unemployment, deteriorating economic conditions, and rampant corruption, as well as

Table 5.4 The predicted value model of Libya's democratic transition

Variables	Collapse transition
Constant	4.44
Transition type	1.02
Region (North Africa and Middle East)	(0.636)
Institutional choice (presidential)	0
Prior regime type (personalistic)	(0.598)
Prior democratic history (none)	0
Per capita GDP	$5,691*0.000254=1.44
GDP growth rate	10.74% * 2.57=0.276
Predicted value of Polity score	**5.94**

Notes

For per capita GDP, we use the most recent data available from the CIA Worldfactbook, listing Libya's 2011 per capita GDP at $5,691. For GDP growth rate, we use a nine-year average based on historical statistics, which equates to 10.74 percent for the years 2001–10.

Where the predicted value equation variables are denoted by zero, this indicates that these variables were used as the baseline category in the OLS model (Table 2). Obtaining the predicted value of the Polity score is achieved through adding or subtracting the values of the variables. Parentheses around a number denote a negative number.

against the government's proposals to modify the constitution to allow Saleh's son to inherit the presidency.

Deteriorating Economic conditions: Yemen is one of the poorest countries in the world with 2011 GDP per capita of $2,648 according to the World Bank. However, political economy approaches can provide some explanations for the causes of the uprising. Economic factors such as poor living conditions and high unemployment were important in contributing to the uprising against Saleh's government. Almost half of the Yemeni population live on $2 or less a day, and one-third suffer from chronic hunger (Finn 2011). At the time of the protests, Yemen had a 35 percent unemployment rate, a 50 percent illiteracy rate, and weak formal institutions outside the largest cities. Political parties were not allowed to freely form and operate. Interior ministers or government committees had to approve the creation of any new party in Yemen (Gelvin 2012, 5).

Popular discontent with *corruption and injustice* under Saleh's 33-year rule is another important cause of the uprising. The power was concentrated in the hands of Saleh's family. Many of his relatives were top military and security commanders, and controlled much of the land and the economy, with large monopolies in various business sectors. Yemen's economy was viewed as a family economy.[10] Yemeni people were discontented with the dictatorial and corrupt government. Inspired by the Arab Spring, the protests in Yemen started in mid-January 2011. Protesters were originally concerned with proposed changes to the constitution, unemployment, poor economic conditions, and corruption but these concerns soon translated into a demand for President Saleh to resign. A mass demonstration of 16,000 protesters took place at the end of January followed by a "Day of Rage" that was held on February 3, 2011. With the resignation of Mubarak in Egypt, more demonstrators were involved in protests that became known as the "Friday of Anger" when thousands of people took part in demonstrations in major cities throughout Yemen.

Social media and the online community played an important role in Yemen as it did in the uprisings that swept the Middle East and North Africa though direct causes of the mass movements were economic conditions, injustice, corruption and grievances. Since Yemen is a poor and largely illiterate country, there are only a small percentage of Internet users. However, 60 percent of the Yemeni population are youth, and they constitute the majority of online users. As radio, television and newspapers were controlled by the government, the youth helped to spread information quickly over the Internet, using Facebook, Twitter, YouTube and blogs, and collaborate on collective actions among anti-government activists and groups in different parts of the country. Various groups even held online meetings, shared information, videos and photos, collaborating with others for rallies, protests, and uprisings.[11]

The Yemeni revolution has ushered in a transition period that ended the old regime and inaugurated a new government to oversee the transition until new elections in 2014. Whether the transition toward democracy will be successful depends on whether or not the new government manages a national dialogue on the amendment of the constitution to create democratic rule and institutions, and provides economic improvements for the population, which are essential to maintaining long-term stability. The following tests the probability of democratic prospects in Yemen.

In running a predicted value simulation for Yemen's tentative transition towards democracy, we assumed the following: (1) Yemen's transitional process can best be characterized as cooperative; (2) it adopts a presidential system of government; (3) its prior regime type is personalistic; and (4) we use Yemen's 2011 per capita GDP and a ten-year GDP growth rate average (2001–10). The predicted values of Yemen's transition by cooperative pact results in an average Polity score over ten years of 6.80, assuming a presidential system of government, an average growth rate of 10.74 percent and per capita GDP of $5,691.

Prospects

Since the toppling of these dictatorships, all four countries have conducted elections, and millions of people can now freely express their political opinions. At the same time, however, these countries still face great uncertainty and daunting challenges. In Libya, the July 2012 elections represented a remarkable achievement for the state after decades of brutal dictatorship. The writing of a constitution in Libya will likely be hampered by divisions between tribes in different parts of the country. Yemen also faces serious challenges. Following mass uprising, turbulence and crackdown throughout 2011, Saleh eventually stepped down, and agreed to transfer power to his vice-president, Abed Rabbo Mansour Hadi. But in the subsequent presidential election, Hadi was the only candidate in the ballot. His weak government is now grappling with a Shiite rebellion in the

Table 5.5 The predicted value model of Yemen's democratic transition

Variables	Cooperative transition
Constant	4.44
Transition type	2.91
Region (North Africa and Middle East)	(0.636)
Institutional choice (presidential)	0
Prior Regime Type (personalistic)	(0.598)
Prior democratic history (none)	0
Per capita GDP	$2,648*0.000254=0.672
GDP growth rate	2.49% * 2.57=0.064
Predicted value of Polity score	**6.80**

Notes
For per capita GDP, we use the most recent data available from the World Bank, listing Yemen's 2011 per capita GDP at $2,648. For GDP growth rate, we use a ten-year average based on historical statistics, which equates to 2.49 percent for the years 2001–10.

Where the predicted value equation variables are denoted by zero, this indicates that these variables were used as the baseline category in the OLS model (Table 2). Obtaining the predicted value of the Polity score is achieved through adding or subtracting the values of the variables. Parentheses around a number denote a negative number.

north, a secessionist movement and an al Qaeda insurgency in the south, and militias and tribes that control substantial parts of the territory. All signs indicate that violence will persist and the economy will remain in trouble. Egypt recently held the first competitive presidential election in its history, but the country does not have an easy path to stability and prosperity. President Mohamed Morsi of the Muslim Brotherhood was ousted by the Supreme Council of the Armed Forces under great pressure after weeks-long mass public demonstrations. Political instability and a difficult period of civil-military relations will continue to cloud the future. Tunisia has emerged as one of the few success stories in the region. Political leaders of different forces have supported moderation, civil liberties and the rule of law. The press is free, civil society has blossomed and the leadership is tackling corruption. Although Tunisia faces some of the same problems as its neighbors, such as a weak state and a challenge from radical Salafists, at least for now, the country is moving in the right direction. However, the future of other countries in the region does not look promising in the short term (Jones 2013).

Will the Arab Spring lead to successful democracies? Many pessimistic views about fledgling democracies in the region are widespread over the media and among academics. However, Sheri Berman of Columbia University argues that the skepticism is misguided. In her discussion on the promises of the Arab Spring, she notes that every wave of democratization over the last century – the second wave after World War I and the third wave after World War II – has been accompanied by widespread questioning of the viability and even desirability of democratic governance in the countries that made a transition from authoritarianism. Berman argues that the critics of democracy ignore the dynamics, turmoil and violence after transition that are inherited from the previous regime. The problems are not evidence of the inherent dysfunctionality of democracy itself, but of the immaturity or irrationality of a particular population, and the fault and legacies of the previous dictatorships. The critics interpret posttransition violence, corruption, confusion and incompetence as signs that particular countries (or even entire regions or religions) are not ready for democracy, as if normal democratic transitions always lead smoothly and directly to stable democratic outcomes. In fact, stable democracy usually emerges only at the end of long, often violent struggles, with many twists, turns, false starts, and detours. Stable democracy requires more than just a shift in political forms; it also involves eliminating the antidemocratic social, cultural and economic legacies of the old regime. Such a process takes lots of time and effort.

Historically, most initial transitions have been the beginning of the democratization process, not the end of it. Most countries that are stable liberal democracies today had a very difficult time getting there. Even the cases most often held up as exemplars of early democratization, such as England and the United States, encountered far more problems than are remembered, with full-scale civil wars along the way. Just as those troubles did not mean democracy was wrong or impossible for North America or Western Europe, so the troubles of today's fledgling Arab democracies do not mean it is wrong or impossible for the Middle

East. The toppling of a longstanding authoritarian regime is not the end of a process but the beginning of it. Even failed democratic experiments are usually positive stages in the political development of countries, and eras in which they get started on rooting out the antidemocratic social, cultural, and economic legacies of the past. Violent and tragic events such as the French Revolution, the collapse of interwar Italian and German democracy, and the American Civil War were not evidence that the countries in question could not create or sustain liberal democracies; they were crucial parts of the process by which those countries achieved just such an outcome. The widespread pessimism about the fate of the Arab Spring is almost certainly misplaced. Therefore Berman believes that the year 2011 was the dawn of a promising new era for the region, and it will be looked on down the road as a historical watershed, even though the rapid downstream will be turbulent, just as the democratic transitions were about France, Italy, Germany, and every other country that supposedly was better off under tyranny (Berman 2013).

The success of democratization will ultimately rest on the success of the economy in these countries; just as poverty and unemployment were the drivers of uprisings that brought down a dictator, so too could they drive protests against a democratic government. Although the relationship between economic development and democracy is subject to debate, the two are indeed correlated (Masoud 2011).

China

The close relationship between economic development and democratic development is the core hypothesis of modernization theory that has been verified repeatedly by rich empirical studies, i.e., the better to do a nation, the more likely the nation is to become democratic. For the past 30 years, China's economy has grown more than nine percent a year, and over ten percent in the past few years. The result is that China's economy has doubled its size to around $5.87 trillion (*The Economist* online, August 16, 2010). China's rapid economic growth, urbanization, and industrialization have made it the second largest economy in the world, and it is predicted that China's share of the world GDP will match the United States in 2020 and surpass it in 2030 (See Table 5.6).

According to the World Bank (2012), China's contribution to global economic growth between 1980 and 2000 was 14 percent and increased to 31 percent between 2010–13. China is also the largest exporter and second largest importer of goods in the world. The *China Daily* reports "China's strong economic growth and its demand for imports are important factors in the stabilization of the global economy" (July 24, 2010). China is the largest creditor nation in the world and owns approximately 20.8 percent of all foreign-owned U.S. Treasury securities.[12] Additionally, China overtook the U.S. as the largest recipient of foreign direct investment (over $100 billion in 2010)[13] and produces two-thirds of the world's photocopiers, 50 percent of its DVD players, 70 percent of cement, 40 percent of socks, one-third of desktop computers, and 25 percent of

Table 5.6 China's share of world GDP

	1995	2007	2020	2030
U.S.	21.7	19.4	18.3	16.6
China	5.5	10.1	17.7	22.7
Japan	8.3	6.0	4.6	3.6
India	3.1	4.3	6.9	8.7
Russia	2.8	2.9	3.1	2.7
EU-27	24.5	20.8	18.6	15.6
Germany	5.3	3.9	3.2	2.5
UK	3.4	3.1	2.9	2.5
France	3.6	3.0	2.5	2.1

Source: Economist Intelligence Unit.

its mobile phones. Indeed, China has become a world factory.[14] It is estimated by China Global Trade and other sources that China will overtake the U.S. in size, measured by GDP, as the world's largest economy between 2016 and 2017.[15]

However, China's phenomenal economic growth has not promoted democracy, and China remains authoritarian despite all the changes in the past decades, which is contradictory to modernization theory and the examples of other modernized nations in Asia and other regions around the world. Therefore, the "Chinese miracle" has puzzled Western observers. This begs the questions: why has democracy not followed modernization in China and why does it seem to lag behind economic development? Is democracy possible in China? If possible, why, and how might it happen?

The answer to the puzzle can be provided by analyzing the factors that are unfavorable and set constraints on democratic development in China and what factors are favorable in the future. Despite the close relationship between economic development and democracy, three major factors are unfavorable to democratic transition in China: successful economic performance, the role of the state in economic development, and institutional constraints.

1   Good economic performance has increased the government's credibility and legitimacy. Successful economic development is considered important for regime performance, and increases the credibility, popular support and legitimacy of the authoritarian regime among the general population. However, it decreases the appeal by the political elite and various social forces of supporting democratic reform and regime change. *The 2008 Pew Global Attitudes Survey in China* indicates that 86 percent of the population was highly satisfied with China's economic performance, 81 percent with their family life, 64 percent with their jobs, and 58 percent with their income. The improved living standards have increased legitimacy for the party-state. Political elites and much of the population do not think it is necessary to promote democracy in order to achieve economic development and

improvements in living standards. Further, they are concerned with the uncertainty and potential instability democracy may create for China. Such concerns are popular even among intellectuals and college students, and many Chinese scholars question the applicability and desirability of democracy for China (Wang Shaoguang; Zheng Yongnian).[16]

2   The role of the state in the economy and the political elite's response to democratic reform play an important role in political development. China's economic reform and development are regime-led and a government-dominated process. The Chinese government not only defines the nature, scope, content and direction of market reform, but also takes the lead to develop the economy, and is heavily involved in organizing and running economic activities by controlling and monopolizing the major economic, financial, social and organizational resources. Government control over political and economic resources enables political elites to cumulate wealth and increase power, and thus decreases their incentives for democratic reform. Therefore the state seems to counteract the positive effects of economic development on democratic development.

3   Institutional constraints play an important role in the political development. China is a Leninist party-state, and it remains unchanged despite market-oriented reform over the past three decades. The party-state has learned how to adjust its ruling methods and has adapted to new situations brought about by economic and social change. The party-state apparatus skillfully penetrates and incorporates the society, and enhances its governability while, at the same time, the party-state increases the dependency of society on the state.

(1)   The business and social elite, and even intellectuals, become heavily dependent upon the state for preferential benefits and sponsorship in their activities. Business and social organizations have to cooperate with the government in order to survive and grow, and intellectuals have to apply for government funds for research projects and programs designed and controlled by the party-state institutions at all levels. Colleges and universities are still run by the state, led by the party organizations and closely monitored by the party-state. Structural and institutional environment ("institutional and contextual setting") affects the relationship between economic development and democratic development, which has been set and defined by the party-state. The Chinese Communist Party has become conservative, rather than radical as in earlier times. The party-state has been less willing to support democratic reform, but more concerned with stability and maintaining the status quo.

(2)   Labor forces and social organizations in a state controlled economic development are less organized and less autonomous of the state, and to a larger degree their growth is dependent upon the state's approval, material benefits, policy permission and sponsorship. Labor and social

elites believe that their interests are better served by maintaining collaborative relationships with the state, and their activities are closely monitored and controlled by the party-state power, and they are politically embedded in the formal and informal institutional structures of the government, and become dependent on the state. Thus, the state has more capability to control and shape the political effects of socioeconomic development on the political system.

(3) Capitalists and the middle classes are also not independent of the state, but dependent on it, creating a powerful network embedded in the institutions and structures of the party-state. In the transition from the centrally planned economy to market economy, capitalists have developed their business by seeking their agents in the government, as political elites control resources and market entry and the private sector's growth is dependent on the state policy, approval, licensing, intervention, administrative and organizational control, and resources, etc.

The above factors pull back the wheel of democratic development despite modernization and economic success, and this explains why democracy lags behind economic development. However, there are also some factors favorable to democratic transition in China in the near future, or at least making democracy possible in the long run:

1   Grassroots election and self-government practice over the past decades, led and controlled by the party-state, has in fact reshaped the political culture, and in particular increased citizens' concept of rights and participation. From rural to urban China, peasants and residents have increasingly participated in local elections, community self-government and local governance of public affairs. There are over 600,000 villagers' committees in rural China and 100,000 neighborhood resident committees in urban China. There has been increasing public unrest, protest and lawsuits against the government for the violation of their rights, well-being and arbitrary use of power by local officials. All these changes have positive effects on political development from below, and both challenge and pressure the government to listen to the people's voice and public opinion.

2   Modernization has brought about social, economic, and cultural changes in China, and reshaped the people's way of living and thinking (modernity). People are beginning to request that the government inform them why certain policies are initiated and implemented, challenge unpopular government policies, and seek to participate in the conduct of public affairs and influence policy making or policy changes. Socioeconomic conditions and social values are quite different than under Mao or imperial rule. People no longer believe whatever the government tells them to believe, and they are beginning to question the official ideology in public or on the Internet. People are increasingly critical of the government's behavior and activities.

3   The third wave of democratization in the age of globalization and new technology has dramatically influenced many Chinese people's reverie about freedom, rights and democracy. One billion *Netizens* have openly and skillfully used Internet blogs, other social media, and cell phones to express their critical views and discontent, communicate views, exchange information, and comment on domestic and international events despite the fact that the party-state has controlled and manipulated the Internet to stifle political communication. The booming social media often influences government policy making, but more importantly, spreads new ideas of freedom, rights and democracy around the nation.

If democracy is possible in the future, we are interested in understanding and predicting how it might happen, and how the modes of transition would impact the outcome. Among the three modes of democratic transition studied in this book, we believe China is more likely to take the middle way towards democracy. China's route has started from below, through grassroots election and self-government practice, but such progress has been carefully controlled and governed by the party-state. Grassroots elections and community self-government practices have fostered citizenship and civic cultures. Under pressure from below, the elites may begin to implement changes from above and finally, at the third phase, proceed through a combination of both forces to democratize China. The timing of transition might be the 20th Party Congress, about ten years from now, as the power succession will be most likely to fuel a power struggle on the top, and thus trigger political crisis needed for a democratic transition.

China has remained a party-state. The Communist Party of China (CPC) is allowing village and community elections yet it tolerates no opposition to its continued rule at different levels of the government. As a powerful party-state regime, it will be more likely to transition in a peaceful manner, either through an elite-led conversion or a cooperative transition. We will examine the implications of both transition types on China's potential democratic success through predictive probability analysis.

Although we can determine Polity scores (the dependent variable) for China at any of the intervals listed in Table 2.0, we use model 4 (the ten-year Polity average) as substantively it is the most meaningful. Through a predicted value equation we determine China's average Polity rating ten years after a hypothetical democratic transition. We make the following assumptions: (1) China will transition peacefully, either through an elite led conversion or through a cooperative pact; (2) it will adopt a presidential system of government; (3) its prior regime type is single party; and (4) we use China's 2012 per capita GDP and a ten-year GDP growth rate average (2003–12).

The predicted values of Table 5.7 show that if China transitions to democracy by conversion, we can expect an average Polity score over ten years of 4.97, assuming a presidential system of government, a steady growth rate of 9.99 percent and per capita GDP of $9,210. Alternatively if China transitions by

Table 5.7 The predicted value model of China's potential democratic transition

	Predicted value I	*Predicted value II*
Variables:	*Conversion*	*Cooperative*
Constant	4.44	4.44
Transition type	0	2.91
Region (Asia)	(0.755)	(0.755)
Institutional choice (presidential)	0	0
Prior regime type (single party)	(1.31)	(1.31)
Prior democratic history (no)	0	0
Per capita GDP	$9,210* 0.000254=2.34	$9,210* 0.000254=2.34
GDP growth rate	9.99% * 2.57=0.256	9.99% * 2.57=0.256
Predicted value of Polity score	**4.97**	**7.88**

Notes
The predicted value model is based on the OLS regression results in Table 2.0. For China's potential transition, we assume the adoption of presidentialism as institutional choice. We also note that China does not have a prior democratic history and, in its current state, will transition as a single party regime.

For per capita GDP, we use the most recent data available from the World Bank, listing China's 2012 per capita GDP at $9,210. For GDP growth rate, we use a ten-year average based on historical statistics from the World Bank, which equates to 9.99%.

Where the predicted value equation variables are denoted by zero, this indicates that these variables were used as the baseline category in the OLS model (Table 2). Obtaining the predicted value of the Polity score is achieved through adding or subtracting the values of the variables. Parentheses around a number denote a negative number.

cooperative pact, the ten-year average Polity score increases significantly from 4.97 to 7.88, a 58 percent increase. Most striking about these results is the profound impact that mode of transition exerts on democratic quality. In China, the difference between a converted transition and a cooperative transition is the difference between a country struggling to become democratic (albeit a great improvement over their current Polity score of –7) to a country moving towards democratic consolidation with a Polity rating in excess of 7.

The larger goal of the predicted value probability laid out in this chapter is to consider the three essential processes to democratization – to understand where a state came from (what were its preconditions – prior regime type, historical GDP growth level), how it transitioned (conversion, cooperation, collapse or foreign intervention) and to determine where it might be heading (consolidation or backsliding). As we have argued throughout, the goal of the successful transition it to lead to an ideal end point, that of democratic consolidation.

Notes

1 Comments from the Oval Office address on the start of military action in Iraq. March 19, 2003.
2 Nadia Al-Sakkaf, "Yemen's Revolution: The Lack of Public Reasoning," accessed online on August 6, 2013 at www.ps.boell.org/downloads/Yemen_public_reasoning_article__Nadia_Al_Sakkaf.pdf.

3 Country Report, "Egypt," *Middle Eastern & Central Asian Studies*, vol. 7, 2011, pp. 1–28.
4 United Nations Human Development Report, "Introducing the Egypt Human Development Report 2010," accessed on August 6, 2013 from www.undp.org.eg/Default. aspx?tabid=227.
5 Michael Slackman, "Reign of Egypt's Mubarak marked by poverty, corruption, despair," *New York Times*, http://o.seattletimes.nwsource.com/html/nation-world/2014070735_egyptmubarak29.html.
6 Ammar Maleki, "Uprisings in the Region and Ignored Indicators." February 9, 2011, accessed August 6, 2013 at: www.payvand.com/news/11/feb/1080.html.
7 Transparency International. Accessed on August 6, 2013 from www.transparency.org/cpi2010/results.
8 "Gaddhafi's Stolen Billions Stashed in London." *Montreal Gazette*, February 25, 2011.
9 The Libyan Intelligence Group, "From a single rodent to many: Corruption in Libya continues to breed post-Gaddafi," accessed August 6, 2013 at: http://libyaintelligence. org/content/single-rodent-many-corruption-libya-continues-breed-post-gaddafi.
10 http://armiesofliberation.com/archives/2010/01/08/yemens-economy-is-a-family-business/.
11 Alakbhar, "Social Media in Yemen: Expecting the Unexpected," December 31, 2011. Accessed on August 6, 2013 from http://english.al-akhbar.com/node/2931.
12 "Major Foreign holders of U.S. Treasury Securities," *U.S. Treasury Department*, accessed on August 6, 2013 from: www.treasury.gov/resource-center/data-chart-center/tic/Documents/mfh.txt.
13 "China nets $100 billion FDI in 2012 despite gradual decline," *Business Standard*, retrieved from: www.business-standard.com/article/international/china-nets-100-billion-fdi-in-2012-despite-gradual-decline-112121800597_1.html.
14 "Engaging China: the Realities for Australian Businesses," The Australian Business Foundation, accessed on August 6, 2013 from: www.nswbusinesschamber.com.au/NSWBC/media/Misc/Ask%20Us%20How/Enaging-China.pdf.
15 China Global Trade.com accessed on August 6, 2013 at www.chinaglobaltrade.com/fact/real-gdp-us-and-china-1980–2030.
16 Wang Shaoguang, "A Chinese Alternative is Possible," www.guancha.cn/wangshao-guang/2013_07_17_158742.shtml.
   Zheng Yongnian, "Where will the "Western Democracy lead China?" retrieved from: www.guancha.cn/zheng-yong-nian/2013_07_09_156858.shtml.

References

Adbulla, K.M. 1999. "The State in Oil Rentier Economies: The Case of Bahrain." In *Change and Development in the Gulf*, ed. Abdelkarim. New York: St. Martin's Press, 51–78.
Alimi, Eitan Y. and David S. Meyer. 2012. "Seasons of Change: Arab Spring and Political Opportunities." *Swiss Political Science Review* 17(4).
Al-Naqeeb, K.H. 1990. *Society and State in the Gulf and Arab Peninsula: A Different Perspective*. New York: Routledge.
Atef, Said. 2009. "Egypt Labor Erupting." Available online: www.solidarity-us.org/node/2365.
Bakry Mohamed Eljack El Medni. 2012. "Civil Society and Democratic Transformation in Contemporary Egypt: Premises and Promises." University of Delaware. Retrieved from ProQuest Dissertations and Theses.
Barany, Zoltan. 2011. "The Role of the Military." *Journal of Democracy* 22(4).

Berman, Sheri. 2013. "The Promise of the Arab Spring." *Foreign Affairs* vol. 92, no. 1: 64–74.

Blechman, Barry and Stephan Kaplan. 1978. *Force without War*. Washington, DC: Brookings.

Borgan, Julian. 2010. "Tunisian President Vows to Punish Rioters after Worst Unrest in a Decade." Available online: www.theguardian.com/world/2010/dec/29/tunisian-president-vows-punish-rioters

Brynen, Rex, Pete W. Moore, Bassell F. Saloukh and Marie-Joelle Zahar. 2012. *Beyond the Arab Spring: Authoritarianism and Democratization in the Arab World*. Boulder, CO: Lynne Rienner Publishers.

Central Intelligence Agency. *The World Factbook* (multiple years). Available online: www.cia.gov/cia/publications/factbook/index.html.

Country Report. 2011. "Egypt." *Middle Eastern & Central Asian Studies* vol. 7: 1–28.

Crystal, Jill. 1990. *Oil and Politics in the Gulf: Rulers and Merchants in Kuwait and Qatar*. New York: Cambridge University Press.

Diamond, Larry. 2003. "Can Iraq Become a Democracy?" *Hoover Digest*, Spring Issue (2).

Diamond, Larry. 2005. "Building Democracy after Conflict: Lessons from Iraq." *Journal of Democracy* 16(1): 9–23.

Diani, Mario. 2011. "Networks and Internet into Perspective." *Swiss Political Science Review*, vol. 17, no. 4: 469–474.

DuPont, Cedric and Florence Passey. 2012. *Swiss Political Science Review*. Swiss Political Science Association vol. 18(1): 101–104.

El-Khawas, Mohamed A. 2012. "Tunisia's Jasmine Revolution: Causes and Impact." *Mediterranean Quarterly* 23(4): 1–23.

Energy Information Administration. United States Department of Energy. 2012. *Country Analysis Briefs: Iraq*. Available online: www.eia.doe.gov/emeu/cabs/iraq.html. February 1, 2013.

Evans, Peter B., Dietrich Rueschemeyer and Theda Skocpol, eds. 1985. *Bringing the State Back In*. Cambridge: Cambridge University Press.

Finn, Tom. 2011. "Yemenis Take to the Streets Calling for President Saleh To Step Down." *The Guardian*, January 27, 2011, London.

Gelvin, James L. 2012. *The Arab Uprisings: What Everyone Needs to Know*. New York: Oxford University Press.

Ghitis, Frida. 2012. "Why Liberals Won in Libya, and Why It Matters." *World Politics Review*, July 19: 1

Ghonim, Wail. 2012. *Revolution 2.0: The Power of the People Is Greater than the People in Power: A Memoir*. Boston: Houghton Mifflin Harcourt.

Ghosh, Bobby. 2011. "The Qaddafi Regime is Broken–What will Take its Place?" *Time International* (Atlantic Edition), vol. 178, issue 9, September 5.

Glanz, James. 2007. "Billions in Oil Missing in Iraq, US Study Says." *New York Times*. www.globalpolicy.org/security/oil/2007/0512billionsoil.htm. May 12.

Goldstone, Jack A. 2012. "Cross-Class Coalitions and the Making of the Arab Revolts of 2011." *Swiss Political Science Review* 17(4): 457–462.

Goodwin, Jeff. 2011. "Why We Were Surprised (Again) by the Arab Spring." *Swiss Political Science Review* 17(4): 452–456.

Gylfason, Thorvaldur. 2001. "Natural Resources, Education, and Economic development." *European Economic Review* 45(4–6): 847–859.

Haerens, Margaret and Lynn M. Zott, eds. 2013. *The Arab Spring*. Farmington Hills, MI: Greenhaven Press: 19–21.

Haggard, Stephan and Robert R. Kaufman. 1995. *The Political Economy of Democratic Transitions*. New Jersey: Princeton University Press: 7–8.

Haggard, Stephan and Robert R. Kaufman. 1997. "The Political Economy of Democratic Transitions." *Comparative Politics*, vol. 29, no. 3: 263–284.

Hamdy, Hassan A. 2011. "Civil Society in Egypt under the Mubarak Regime." *Afro-Asian Journal of Social Sciences*, vol. 2, no. 2.2, Quarter II: 3–4.

Harb, Imad. 2003. "The Egyptian Military in Politics: Disengagement or Accommodation?" *Middle East Journal*, vol. 57, no. 2: 269–285.

Herman, Edward and Frank Brodhead. 1984. *Demonstration Elections*. Boston: South End Press.

Hermann, Margaret and Charles Kegley. 1996. "Ballots, a Barrier against the Use of Bullets and Bombs." *Journal of Conflict Resolution* 40(3): 436–460.

Howard, Philip N. and Muzammil M. Hussain. 2011. "The Role of Digital Media." *Journal of Democracy*, vol. 22, no. 3: 36–37.

Huntington, Samuel P. 1991. *The Third Wave: Democratization in the Late Twentieth Century*. Norman: University of Oklahoma Press.

Inayatullah, Sohail. 2011. "The Arab Spring: What's Next?" *World Affairs* 15(3): 36–46.

Joffé, George. 2011. "The Arab Spring In North Africa: Origins And Prospects." *Journal of North African Studies*, vol. 16, no. 4: 507–532.

Jones, Seth G. 2013. "The Mirage of the Arab Spring." *Foreign Affairs*, vol. 92, no. 1, 2013: 55–63.

Kamrava, Mehran. 2007. "The Middle East's Democracy Deficit in Comparative Perspective." *Perspectives on Global Development & Technology*, vol. 6: 193–194.

Karl, Terry Lynn. 1987. "Petroleum and Political Pacts: The Transition to Democracy in Venezuela." *Latin American Research Review* 22(1): 63–94.

Karl, Terry Lynn. 1990. "Dilemmas of Democratization in Latin America." *Comparative Politics* 23(1): 1–22.

Khouri, Rami G. 2013. "The Arab Spring Was Triggered by a Desire for Democracy and Social Justice." In *The Arab Spring*, ed. Margaret Haerens and Lynn M. Zott. Detroit: Greenhaven Press: 1–3.

Krasner, Stephen D. 1988. "Sovereignty: An Institutional Perspective." *Comparative Political Studies*, vol. 21: 66–94.

Lawson, Chappell and Strom C. Thacker. 2003. "Democracy? Iraq?" *Hoover Digest* (3): Summer Issue. Online version.

Lowenthal, Abraham. 1991. "The United States and Latin American Democracy: Learning from History." In *Exporting Democracy: Themes and Issues,* ed. A. Lowenthal. Baltimore, MD: Johns Hopkins University Press: 243–246.

Lust, Ellen. 2012. "Change and Continuity in Elections after the Arab Uprisings." *Swiss Political Science Review* vol. 18, no. 1: 110 –113.

Lynch, Marc. 2012. *Arab Uprising: The Unfinished Revolutions of the Middle East.* New York, NY: Public Affairs.

Maddy-Weitzman, Bruce. 2011. "Tunisia's Morning After." *Middle East Quarterly* 18.3 (2011): 11–17.

March, James G. and Johan P. Olsen. 1984. "The New Institutionalism: Organizational Factors in Political Life." *American Political Science Review* vol. 78: 734 –749.

Masoud, Tarek. 2011. "The Road to (and from) Liberation Square." *Journal of Democracy* vol. 22, no. 3: 20–34.

Meernik, James. 1996. "United States Military Intervention and the Promotion of Democracy." *Journal of Peace Research* 33(4): 391–402.

Mekay, Emad. 2011. "One Libyan Battle Is Fought in Social and News Media." February 23, 2011. Retrieved from: www.nytimes.com/2011/02/24/world/middleeast/24iht-m24libya.html?_r=0.

Miller, Laurel E., Jeffrey Martini, F. Stephen Larrabee, Angel Rasaba, Stephanie Pezard, Julie E. Taylor and Tewodaj Mengistu. 2012. *Democratization in the Arab World: Prospects and Lessons from Around the Globe*. Santa Monica, CA: RAND Corporation: 70.

Najmabadi, A. 1987. "Iran's Turn to Islam: From Modernism to Moral Order." *Middle East Journal* 41(2): 202–217.

Nepstad, Sharon Erickson. 2011. "Nonviolent Resistance in the Arab Spring: The Critical role of Military-Opposition Alliances," *Swiss Political Science Review* 17(4): 485–491.

Noueihed, Lin and Alex Warren. 2012. *Battle for the Arab Spring: Revolution, Counterrevolution, and the Making of a New Era*. Yale University Press: 308.

O'Neil, Patrick H. 1996. "Revolution from Within: Institutional Analysis, Transitions from Authoritarianism, and the Case of Hungary." *World Politics* vol. 48 (July1996): 579–603.

Paciello, Maria Cristina. 2011. *Tunisia: Changes and Challenges of Political Transition*. Brussels, Belgium: MEDPRO, Technical Report no. 3.

Papyrakis, Elissaios and Reyer Gerlagh. 2002. "The Resource Curse Hypothesis and Its Transmission Channels." Study for the IVM, Institute of Environmental Studies, Vrje Universiteit, Amsterdam.

Peceny, Mark. 1999. "Forcing Them To Be Free." *Political Research Quarterly* 52(3): 549–582.

Plattner, Marc F. 2011. "The Global Context." *Journal of Democracy* vol. 22, no. 4: 5–12.

Powell, Walter W. and Paul J. DiMaggio, eds. 1991. *The New Institutionalism in Organizational Analysis*. Chicago: University of Chicago Press.

Pridham, Geoffrey and Tatu Vanhanen, eds. 1994. *Democratization in Eastern Europe: Domestic and International Perspectives*. New York: Routledge.

Przeworski, Adam. 1991. *Democracy and the Market: Political and Economic Reforms in Eastern Europe and Latin America*. New York: Cambridge University Press.

Rosenau, James. 1969. "Intervention as a Scientific Concept." *Journal of Conflict Resolution* 12(2): 149–171.

Sachs, Jeffrey D. and Andrew M. Warner. 1995. "Natural Resource Abundance and Economic Growth." *NBER Working Paper No. 5398*. Cambridge, MA: National Bureau of Economic Research.

Schlumberger, Oliver and Torsten Matzke. 2012. "Path toward Democracy? The Role of Economic Development." *Swiss Political Science Review* 18(1): 105–109.

Schumacher, Tobias. 2012. "Gulf Cooperation Council Countries and Yemen." In *The European Union and the Arab Spring: Promoting Democracy and Human Rights in the Middle East*, ed. Joel Peters. Lanham: Lexington Press: 109–126.

Skocpol, T. 1982. "Rentier State and Shi'a Islam in the Iranian Revolution." *Theory and Society* 11: 265–283.

Springborg, Robert. 2011. "The Political Economy of the Arab Spring." *Mediterranean Politics* vol. 16, no. 3: 427–433.

Steinmo, Sven, Kathleen Thelen and Frank Longstrth, eds. 1992. *Structuring Politics: Historical Institutionalism in Comparative Analysis*. Cambridge, Cambridge University Press.

Stepan, Alfred. 2012. "Tunisia's Transition and Twin Tolerations." *Journal of Democracy* vol. 23, no. 2: 89–103.

Thiel, Tobias. 2012. "After the Arab Spring: Power Shift in the Middle East?: Yemen's Arab Spring: from Youth Revolution to Fragile Political Transition." IDEAS reports – special reports, Kitchen, Nicholas, ed. SR011. LSE IDEAS, London School of Economics and Political Science, London, UK.

UNDP. "Introducing the Egypt Human Development Report 2010." Retried from www.undp.org.eg/Default.aspx?tabid=227.

Vira, Varun and Anthony H. Cordesman 2011. "The Libyan Uprising: An Uncertain Trajectory." Center for Strategic and International Studies, 20 June 2011: 66. Available online: http://csis.og/files/publication/110620_libya.pdf

Whitehead, Laurence. 1991. "The Imposition of Democracy." In *Exporting Democracy: Volume One: Themes and Issues,* ed. Laurence Whitehead. Baltimore: The Johns Hopkins University Press: 216–242.

6 Conclusion

Starting with the American and French Revolutions in the late eighteenth century, representative government became a lasting reality for the first time in thousands of years. Fueled by the American experience and the ideas put forth in the Revolution, numerous countries around the world started a slow but steady progress towards democracy. The result was profound, a gradual demise of long-held monarchies and brutal dictatorships. In western European countries, where a plethora of philosophical thoughts of what constitutes just and unjust regimes emerged, the transition to democracy gained momentum. Over the next few hundred years and continuing to this day, the transformation of political systems around the world saw the collapse of dictatorial regimes in favor of a system of rule by the people.

All of these transitions, however, did not come easy and a high price was paid. The sacrifices of those who held strong beliefs in freedom of rule gave much in their quest for democracy, most notably their lives. The "Tomb of the Unknown Soldier" situated in Independence Square, Philadelphia contains a profound saying *"Freedom is a Light for which many men have died in darkness."* Indeed, for those nations that are now democratic and those that continue to struggle for freedom, the movement away from the darkness that surrounds dictatorship towards the light of freedom is perhaps the greatest progression that humankind has ever made for it touches the very foundation of our existence.

Today there are more democratic nations in the world than ever before and it appears that the global democratic revolution is not likely to stop until every country around the globe is governed by a democratic polity. Even in nations such as Libya and Egypt where democracy seemed improbable just ten years ago, the citizens are demanding greater rights and a voice in government. For students of democratization, the progression of the nation-state from authoritarianism to free government generated a variety of questions. The logic of the inquiry appropriately started with concerns and exploration into the mechanisms that cause states to become democratic and then progressed into questions of how to stay democratic. That is, it is not enough to merely undergo the process of transition. Although the transition is a necessary step towards democracy, the larger question is how to remain democratic. The central research questions focused on the process of regime change itself and its exertion on helping a country remain free.

In moving from dictatorship to democracy, the core of governmental change is characterized by the transformation of the body politic from repression to freedom. In this study, regime transitions "imply the movement from something toward something else" (O'Donnell and Schmitter 1986, 65). That is the change from one kind of regime to another – a change in kind. According to Lawson (1993), "regimes embody the norms and principles of the political organization of the state, which are set out in the rules and procedures within which governments operate" (187).[1] The key to the definition of "regime" here is directly related to the values embodied in the principles and norms. A change of government does not necessarily involve a change of regime if governments formed within or under a particular regime are all essentially of the same character to the extent that these governments share a commitment or conform to the fundamental principles and norms of the regime. Rules and procedures, which can take various forms and are subject to change, derive from and are secondary to principles and norms. A "regime change" is a fundamental change in or abandonment of the principles and norms governing the nature of the regime, distinguished from a "regime weakening", which constitutes a phase in regime change. "Regime weakening" occurs where the relationship between norms, principles, and rules becomes less coherent or where actual practice becomes inconsistent with the values or rules of the regime (Lawson 1993, 185–186). Krasner (1983, 5) has made a clear and useful distinction between three related but different concepts:

> change within a regime involves alterations of rules and decision-making procedures, but not of norms or principles; change of regime involves alteration of norms and principles; and weakening of a regime involves incoherence among the components of the regime or inconsistency between the regime and related behavior.

Although the notion of "regime" in international relations theory is situated in a different context of relationships, the idea that regimes are an embodiment of principles, norms and rules is the key point, and therefore is applicable to the notion of "regime" in both domestic and international arenas (Lawson 1993, 1985).

Democratic transitions, therefore, simply imply the movement away from an authoritarian regime toward a democratic one. There is a large and robust literature on what causes states to transition to democracy, notably rooted in modernization theory. The antecedent variables, however, should not be confounded with the way that states transition as these are two distinct phenomena. Thus, a process of democratization may grow and gain momentum from a variety of endogenous or exogenous factors such as persistent and robust economic growth, a vibrant civil society that leaves the populace demanding a greater voice in government, or a snowballing effect where neighboring states are the impetus to change within another country (e.g., the end of the Cold War and as seen during the events of the Arab Spring). Ultimately, however, political elites themselves must take measures to initiate a transition. Should a growing opposition no longer face repression by incumbent rulers, then there is a greater chance the transition will occur peacefully. Alternatively, a powerful opposition that incumbents continue to marginalize may result in an attempt to violently overthrow the government, often through a mass uprising in the form of a revolution.

In this study, we have been concerned with the mechanisms that transform nation-states into democratic polities. The core research questions were driven by a common theme – what makes democracies succeed and/or fail and does the mode of transition influence the quality of democracy and its duration? To answer these questions, we developed a theory and argued that the mode of transition directly impacts the success and failure of democracy. Consequently, modes of transition matter as they affect both democratic quality and sustainability by creating an environment characterized by cooperation among competing political elites or exclusionary mechanisms that allow a single party or elite to retain a monopoly on power.

Relative power advantages among incumbents and opposition groups during the transitional process are important. Depending on who obtains the upper hand leading into the transitional phase, this will dictate who asserts the most control over the transitional process. Our theory strongly suggests that cooperative transitions, which are more inclusive, would be more likely to create a transition that results in a level playing field for all in order to secure the varied interests of competing forces a place in the new government. Incumbents with a power advantage are less than favorable. Already in power, often for many years, history shows us that they generally attempt to design institutions and electoral rules that guarantee their continued rule, albeit under the banner of democracy.

In the event that incumbent elites refuse to engage in negotiations for governmental reform with a powerful opposition, the result may lead to regime collapse, or revolution. Collapse, however, does not seem to be conducive to successful democracy as one-third of these transitions will eventually fail. Likewise, dictators who tolerate no opposition and hold an extreme power advantage and therefore can only be removed by a dominant external force show mixed results when transitioning. Virtually all the World War II transitions succeeded, while subsequent foreign liberations have been more challenging, such as the difficulties encountered in Afghanistan and Iraq. Yet, regardless of transitional mode, to the extent the transition is characterized by a cooperative atmosphere, where opposition groups and incumbent elites work together toward transitioning the state, democracy has a greater chance of succeeding. In the ideal setting, transitional players compete for policy space rather than struggle to eliminate opposition players (O'Donnell and Schmitter 1986, 72). In a cooperative environment, this is precisely what happens, in addition to players abiding by democratic rules and procedures.

Thus, the empirical analyses strongly suggest that cooperative transitions, where opposition groups work together with incumbent elites to peacefully transition the state, result in democracies that last longer and are associated with higher measures of democratic quality. The character of the transition process emerging from a cooperative transition results in institutional structures (i.e., "getting the institutions right" – the appropriate electoral system, constitution, separation of powers and a military subservient to the civil government to name a few) that are crucial to democratic consolidation as they tend to be more inclusive and provide a level playing field among competing parties. Where opposition groups are more powerful than incumbents yet are willing to come together to transition the state, democracy is likely to flourish. An important finding of this study is that cooperative transitions have only a 5 percent reversion rate; of 37 cooperative transitions since 1900, only two have reverted to dictatorship, whereas transitions led by incumbent elites revert at a rate of almost 50 percent.

The findings in this study also raise some doubts about works by Geddes (1999) and Svolik (2008) who suggested that characteristics of the prior regime determine the path available to democratizing countries and whether or not that country will create a successful democracy. Notably missing from their analyses is information concerning the mode of transition. The cross-national dataset and empirical analyses from this study show that prior regime type is not a robust predictor of democratic survivability. Rather, the mode of transition exerts an independent and profound effect on democracy and the results are statistically significant.

Emerging from the analysis in this chapter is that the mode of transition to democracy exerts an important impact on both the quality and duration of democracy. Further, prior regime type does not appear to be the driving factor towards democratic success. O'Donnell and Schmitter (1986, 65) make an interesting observation, that

> one major source of indeterminacy in the length and outcome of the transition lies in the fact that those factors which were necessary and sufficient for provoking the collapse or self-transformation of an authoritarian regime may be neither necessary or sufficient to ensure the instauration of another regime – at least of all, political democracy.

That is, the causes of transitions do not guarantee a favorable end result. Resulting from the theory laid out in Chapter 3, a cooperative environment to transition facilitates an atmosphere of inclusiveness that satisfies parties competing for power. An important factor for parties and individuals losing in democratic elections following a long period of authoritarianism is that they retain the right to run again in the future and achieve an outcome that is more favorable to them; without this hope, the new democracy may be either dominated by one powerful force or slip into intolerable power struggles that can derail the new democracy. The concern of transition by conversion is that incumbent elites retain a continued grip on power that impedes democratic success.

The Predicted Value Simulation can be run on a variety of countries to demonstrate divergences in potential outcomes. Recent events in the Middle East (i.e., foreign interventions in Afghanistan and Iraq and the more recent Arab Spring provide great variability in calculated predicted probabilities). Generally speaking, we see countries with low per capita GDP, although resource rich, experience violent transitions to democracy with numerous factions (including religious sects) that do not agree democracy is the best outcome for their country. No doubt, these transitions, whether they are ultimately democratic or not, will take years to sort out, but are an important step towards democracy.

A major contribution of this study is the creation of a cross-national dataset of all democratic transitioning states since 1900, and coding them according to the mode of transition, which was accomplished through detailed case study analyses and cross-verification with widely accepted works on transitions. We created a categorization of modes of transition that allows for the placement of any transitioning state into one of four types. To the best of our knowledge, this is the first study to statistically test the impact of mode of transition on the quality and duration of democracy. Existing studies of this issue are almost exclusively case oriented or regionally focused. None use the larger dataset employed in this study and subject it to a rigorous statistical analysis.

Our findings give cause to rethink the role that the mode of transition plays in the sustainability of democracy. By understanding that certain transition modes are likely to be more successful than others provides policymakers and elites a better understanding of the obstacles to successful democracy. We do not suggest that states neatly choose how to transition but knowing that certain transitions face various difficulties brings a greater awareness of potential obstacles. For example, we have learned that cooperative transitions are likely to succeed while converted transitions face many difficulties. China has provided us with a good empirical case in which the regime-led and controlled reform has yielded no result in democratic outcome despite its economic miracle and success in modernization. Understanding the success or failure that is associated with any transition mode allows us to evaluate the obstacles that certain transition types face (e.g., if a state transitions through conversion, then what steps can be taken to ensure democratic success, if any?).

In conclusion, it is our hope that this study returns some attention to the process of democratization and the role that the mode of transition plays in democratic sustainability. Throughout the 1980s and 1990s, there was a large literature on transitional types yet few, if any, generalizable conclusions were reached. Rather, summaries were drawn on a case-by-case or regional basis and therefore, the advancement of our collective knowledge was minimalized. As certain regions began to grapple with consolidation, the transition research was largely set aside. Nonetheless, many regions of the world remain undemocratic – the Middle East, Africa and parts of Asia, particularly China, the largest country with the most rapid economic growth over the past 30 years. We are also seeing slippage in other parts of the world, such as Eastern Europe.

The path to democracy is complex and fully understanding the nuances that create a quality and sustainable democracy requires further research. Future work that builds upon the findings in this study is an important next step, especially detailed case studies of the mechanisms contained within each transitional mode that lead to the success and failure of democracy. Exploring how the cooperative nature of successful democracies leads to an inclusive environment is worthy of additional scholarly inquiry, in addition to identifying the problems associated with the less-than-successful transitions and how this jeopardizes the post-transitional phase. Our end goal is complex yet simple to state – creating democracies that endure. This study is but a small part of that process.

Note

1 For more discussions on the definition of "regime" as well as the distinctions among "state," "regime" and "government," see also Robert M. Fishman, "Rethinking State and Regime: Southern Europe's Transitions to Democracy," *World Politics*, vol. 42, April 1990, p. 428; Peter Calvert, ed., *The Process of Political Succession* (London: Macmillan, 1987), pp. 18, 248; Jan-Erik Lane and Svante O. Ersson, *Politics and Society in Western Europe* (London: Sage, 1987), p. 279; Allan Larson, *Comparative Political Analysis* (Chicago: Nelson Hall, 1980), p. 19; Naomi Chazan, Robert Mortimer, John Ravenhill and Donald Rothchild, *Politics and Society in Contemporary Africa* (London: Macmillan, 1988), p. 17.

References

Geddes, Barbara. 1999. "Authoritarian Breakdown: Empirical Test of a Game Theoretic Approach." *Paper prepared for the annual meeting of the American Political Science Association*, Atlanta, Georgia.

Krasner, Stephen D., ed. 1983. *International Regimes* Ithaca: Cornell University Press.

Lawson, Stephanie. 1993. "Conceptual Issues in the Comparative Study of Regime Change and Democratization." *Comparative Politics* 25(2): 183–205.

O'Donnell, Guillermo and Philippe Schmitter. 1986. *Transitions from Authoritarian Rule: Tentative Conclusions about Uncertain Democracies*. Baltimore: The Johns Hopkins University Press.

Svolik, Milan. 2008. "Authoritarian Reversals and Democratic Consolidation." *American Political Science Review* 102(2): 153–168.

Appendix

Appendix A Democratic transitioning states from 1900 to 1999

Country	Trans yr	Trans type	Prior demhis	PY123a	PY456a	PY5a	PY78910a	PY10a
Australia	1901	2	0	10.00	10.00	10	10.00	10.00
Portugal	1911	3	0	7.00	7.00	7	7.00	7.00
Denmark	1915	1	0	10.00	10.00	10	10.00	10.00
Estonia	1917	3	0	9.00	10.00	9.5	10.00	9.78
Finland	1917	2	0	8.67	10.00	9.2	10.00	9.60
Netherlands	1917	2	0	10.00	10.00	10	10.00	10.00
Sweden	1917	2	0	10.00	10.00	10	10.00	10.00
Czechoslovakia	1918	2	0	7.00	7.00	7	7.00	7.00
Poland	1918	3	0	8.00	8.00	8	2.50	5.80
Germany	1919	3	0	6.00	6.00	6	6.00	6.00
Austria	1920	4	0	8.00	8.00	8	8.00	8.00
Latvia	1920	3	0	7.00	7.00	7	7.00	7.00
Ireland	1921	3	0	8.00	8.00	8	10.00	8.80
Greece	1926	3	1	10.00	10.00	10	9.00	9.60
Colombia	1930	1	1	5.00	5.00	5	5.00	5.00
Spain	1931	3	1	7.00	7.00	7	0.00	4.20
Philippines	1935	1	0	5.00	5.00	5	2.00	4.57
Argentina	1937	1	0	5.00	5.00	5	-8.00	0.67
Belgium	1944	4	1	10.00	10.00	10	10.00	10.00
Finland	1944	4	1	10.00	10.00	10	10.00	10.00
Greece	1944	4	1	8.00	6.67	8	4.00	6.00
Guatemala	1944	3	0	5.00	5.00	5	2.00	3.80
Syria	1944	3	0	5.00	1.00	5	-4.75	-0.10
Austria	1946	4	1	10.00	10.00	10	10.00	10.00
Brazil	1946	1	0	5.67	5.00	5.4	5.00	5.20
France	1946	4	1	10.00	10.00	10	10.00	10.00

continued

Appendix A Continued

Country	Trans yr	Trans type	Prior demhis	PY123a	PY456a	PY5a	PY78910a	PY10a
Turkey	1946	1	0	7.00	7.00	7	5.50	6.40
Israel (state created)	1948		0	10.00	10.00	10	10.00	10.00
Italy	1948	4	0	10.00	10.00	10	10.00	10.00
Burma	1948	2	0	8.00	8.00	8	8.00	8.00
Sri Lanka	1948	2	0	7.00	7.00	7	7.00	7.00
Germany, West	1949	4	1	10.00	10.00	10	10.00	10.00
India	1950	2	0	9.00	9.00	9	9.00	9.00
Philippines	1950	4	1	5.00	5.00	5	5.00	5.00
Japan	1952	4	0	10.00	10.00	10	10.00	10.00
Uruguay	1952	1	0	8.00	8.00	8	8.00	8.00
Sudan	1954	1	0	8.00	-2.00	5	-7.00	-1.00
Syria	1954	3	1	7.00	7.00	7	-3.67	2.43
Chile	1955	1	1	5.00	5.00	5	5.25	5.10
Colombia	1957	3	1	7.00	7.00	7	7.00	7.00
Malaysia	1957	2	0	10.00	10.00	10	10.00	10.00
Laos	1958		0	5.00	–	5	–	5.00
Venezuela	1958	3	0	6.00	6.00	6	6.00	6.00
Jamaica	1959	1	0	10.00	10.00	10	10.00	10.00
Singapore	1959	1	0	7.00	7.00	7	-2.00	2.50
Cyprus	1960	3	0	8.00	–	8	7.00	7.60
Korea, South	1960	3	0	-2.00	3.00	0	3.00	1.50
Nigeria	1960	1	0	8.00	7.33	7.8	-7.00	1.80
Somalia	1960	1	0	7.00	7.00	7	3.50	5.60
Sierra Leone	1961	1	0	6.00	6.00	6	-1.00	3.20
Turkey	1961	3	1	9.00	8.33	8.8	8.00	8.40
Trinidad	1962	2	0	8.00	8.00	8	8.00	8.00
Gambia	1965	1	0	8.00	8.00	8	8.00	8.00
Sudan	1965	3	1	7.00	7.00	7	-7.00	0.00
Botswana	1966	2	0	6.00	7.00	6.4	7.00	6.70

Country	Year							
Lesotho	1966	1	0	9.00	-3.00	5.4	-7.50	-1.20
Mauritius	1968	1	0	9.00	9.00	9	9.00	9.00
Fiji	1970	2	0	9.00	9.00	9	9.00	9.00
Lebanon	1970	1	0	5.00	5.00	5	—	5.00
Bangladesh	1972	1	1	4.67	-7.00	0	-4.00	-2.30
Argentina	1973	1	1	6.00	-9.00	0	-8.50	-4.30
Pakistan	1973	1	1	8.00	-2.00	5	-7.00	-1.00
Turkey	1973	3	0	9.00	9.00	9	-1.50	4.80
Papa New Guinea	1975	2	1	10.00	10.00	10	10.00	10.00
Greece	1975	3	1	8.00	8.00	8	8.00	8.00
Portugal	1976	3	0	9.00	9.00	9	10.00	9.40
Solomon Islands	1978	1	1	7.00	7.00	7	7.00	7.00
Spain	1978	1	0	9.00	9.67	9.2	10.00	9.60
Dominican Republic	1978	2	0	6.00	6.00	6	6.00	6.00
Ecuador	1979	1	1	9.00	8.67	9	8.25	8.60
Nigeria	1979	1	0	7.00	2.33	7	-7.00	0.00
Ghana	1979	3	0	1.67	-7.00	-1.8	-7.00	-4.40
Zimbabwe	1980	1	0	5.00	1.00	3.4	-4.25	0.10
Peru	1980	1	0	7.00	7.00	7	7.00	7.00
Honduras	1982	1	1	6.00	5.00	5.6	5.75	5.60
Bolivia	1982	2	0	8.00	9.00	8.4	9.00	8.70
Turkey	1983	1	1	7.00	7.00	7	9.00	7.80
Argentina	1983	3	1	8.00	8.00	8	7.00	7.60
El Salvador	1984	1	0	6.00	6.00	6	6.75	6.30
Uruguay	1985	2	1	9.00	9.67	9.2	10.00	9.60
Brazil	1985	1	1	7.33	8.00	7.6	8.00	7.80
Sudan	1986	1	1	7.00	-7.00	1.4	-7.00	-2.80
Philippines	1987	3	0	8.00	8.00	8	8.00	8.00
Pakistan	1988	1	1	8.00	8.00	8	7.75	7.90
South Korea	1988	2	0	6.00	6.00	6	6.00	6.00
Poland	1989	2	1	6.00	8.00	6.8	9.00	7.80
Chile	1989	1	1	8.00	8.00	8	8.00	8.00
Panama	1989	4	0	8.00	8.33	8	9.00	8.50

continued

Appendix A Continued

Country	Trans yr	Trans type	Prior demhis	PY123a	PY456a	PY5a	PY78910a	PY10a
Fiji	1990	3	1	5.00	5.00	5	5.25	5.10
Bulgaria	1990	1	0	8.00	8.00	8	8.00	8.00
Hungary	1990	1	0	10.00	10.00	10	10.00	10.00
Czechoslovakia	1990	2	1	8.00	10.00	8.8	10.00	9.40
Nicaragua	1990	2	0	6.00	6.67	6	8.00	7.00
Namibia	1990	3	0	6.00	6.00	6	6.00	6.00
Nepal	1990	2	0	5.00	5.00	5	5.25	5.10
Romania	1990	3	0	5.00	5.00	5	8.00	6.20
Belarus	1991	1	0	7.00	0.00	5.6	-7.00	-0.70
Armenia	1991	1	0	7.00	1.33	6.2	2.25	3.40
Benin	1991	2	0	6.00	6.00	6	6.00	6.00
Lithuania	1991	2	0	10.00	10.00	10	10.00	10.00
Macedonia	1991	2	0	6.00	6.00	6	6.00	6.00
Slovenia	1991	2	0	10.00	10.00	10	10.00	10.00
Ukraine	1991	2	0	6.00	6.33	6	7.00	6.50
Zambia	1991	2	0	6.00	4.33	6	1.00	3.50
Bangladesh	1991	3	1	6.00	6.00	6	6.00	6.00
Estonia	1991	2	1	6.00	6.00	6	6.00	6.00
Latvia	1991	2	1	8.00	8.00	8	8.00	8.00
Moldova	1991	2	0	5.67	7.00	6.2	7.00	6.60
Albania	1992	2	0	5.00	3.33	4	5.00	4.50
Congo Brazzaville	1992	1	1	5.00	1.33	5	-5.75	-0.40
Thailand	1992	3	0	9.00	9.00	9	9.00	9.00
Paraguay	1992	3	0	7.00	7.00	7	6.75	6.90
Congo	1992	1	0	5.00	1.33	5	-5.75	-0.40
Guyana	1992	1	0	6.00	6.00	6	6.00	6.00
Taiwan	1992	1	0	7.00	8.00	7.2	9.00	8.10
Mongolia	1992	2	0	9.00	9.67	9.2	10.00	9.60
Mali	1992	3	0	7.00	6.67	7	6.00	6.50
Niger	1992	1	0	8.00	-1.33	5.2	1.50	2.60

Country	Trans yr	Trans type	Prior demhis	PY123a	PY456a	PY5a	PY78910a	PY10a
Russia	1992	1	0	4.67	4.00	4.4	5.50	4.80
Madagascar	1992	2	0	9.00	8.67	9	7.00	8.10
Central African Republic	1993	2	0	5.00	5.00	5	5.00	5.00
Lesotho	1993	1	1	8.00	8.00	8	8.00	8.00
Slovakia	1993	2	0	7.00	7.67	7	9.00	8.00
Guinea-Bissau	1994	1	0	5.00	5.00	5	3.50	4.25
Mozambique	1994	1	0	6.00	6.00	6	6.00	6.00
Malawi	1994	2	0	7.00	7.00	7	5.75	6.50
South Africa	1994	2	0	9.00	9.00	9	9.00	9.00
Haiti	1994	4	0	7.00	7.00	7	-2.00	3.00
Guatemala	1996	1	1	8.00	8.00	8	8.00	8.00
Indonesia	1999	3	0	7.00	7.00	7	–	7.00

Notes

Transition Type

1 Conversion.
2 Cooperative.
3 Collapse.
4 Foreign intervention.

Coding

Trans yr: transition year.
Trans type: mode of transition (conversion, cooperative, collapse, foreign intervention).
Prior demhis: prior democratic history.
PY123a – average of Polity IV scores for the first three years following the transition.
PY456a – average of Polity IV scores for years 4, 5, and 6 following the transition.
PY5a – average of Polity IV scores for the first five years following the transition.
PY78910a – average of Polity IV scores for years 7, 8, 9, and 10 following the transition.
PY10a – average of Polity IV scores for the ten years following the transition.

Summary Statistics of Transition Type

Conversion: N=48, PY10a=4.60.
Cooperative: N=37, PY10a=7.76.
Collapse: N=31, PY10a=5.84.
Foreign intervention: N=12, PY10a=8.25.

Appendix B Robustness checks

Robustness check 1 OLS regression for democratic quality – 10-year average after transition (robust standard errors)

Independent variable	PY1–10
• Conversion	–
• Cooperative	3.15*** (0.64)
• Collapse	1.23 (0.80
• Foreign intervention	3.77*** (0.88)
Constant robust standard error	4.59*** (0.56)
R^2	0.18
N	128

Notes
Significance levels: *** <0.01; ** <0.05; * <0.10 (two-tailed tests).
Basic model reflects the ten-year Polity average of the dependent variable with no control variables. Baseline category of the dependent variable is conversion.
Dataset includes all democratic transitions since 1900.

Robustness check 2 Duration analysis for democratic longevity – 10 years after transition

Independent variable	Parameter estimate (hazard ratio)	Robust standard error	Risk ratio (z)	P
Transition type				
• Conversion	–	–	–	–
• Cooperative	0.089	0.065	–3.30***	0.001
• Collapse	0.642	0.237	–1.20	0.231
• Foreign intervention	0.294	0.215	–1.67*	0.095

Notes
Number of subjects: 125; number of failures: 36; time at risk=1061; Wald Chi Squared: 13.14; significance levels: *** <0.01; ** <0.05; * <0.10.
The model uses conversion as a baseline transition category.

Robustness check 3 OLS regression for democratic quality – 10 years after transition, additional control for WWII (robust standard errors in parentheses)

Independent variables	(1) PY1–3	(2) PY4–6	(3) PY7–10	(4) PY1–10
Transition type				
• Conversion	–	–	–	–
• Cooperative	0.552 (0.400)	3.16*** (0.849)	4.60*** (1.12)	2.96*** (0.726)
• Collapse	–0.832 (0.583)	2.09* (1.13)	1.90 (1.54)	1.12 (0.957)
• Foreign intervention	0.225 (0.712)	0.951 (1.14)	0.244 (2.584)	0.025 (1.41)
Region				
• Europe	1.01 (0.754)	–0.310 (1.18)	–0.323 (2.05)	0.414 (1.26)
• North Africa and Middle East	1.14 (0.841)	–1.98 (2.03)	–3.70 (3.01)	–1.21 (1.74)
• South America	0.017 (0.580)	–1.17 (1.16)	–1.09 (2.01)	–0.837 (1.21)
• Asia and Pacific	0.170 (0.743)	–1.36 (1.21)	–1.46 (2.02)	–1.14 (1.31)
• Sub-Saharan Africa	–0.060 (0.666)	–1.60 (1.31)	–4.23** (2.02)	–2.45** (1.24)
Institutional choice				
• Parliamentary	0.614 (0.548)	0.623 (0.989)	–0.942 (1.32)	–0.307 (0.873)
• Mixed	0.726 (0.521)	0.329 (1.05)	–0.044 (1.40)	0.419 (0.946)
Prior regime type				
• Single party	–1.60** (0.728)	–1.71 (1.18)	–0.464 (1.73)	–1.29 (1.14)
• Personalistic	–0.579 (0.581)	–1.20 (1.27)	0.728 (1.63)	–0.456 (1.09)
• Previous colony	0.068 (0.723)	–0.093 (1.37)	0.942 (1.96)	0.678 (1.21)
WWII	0.389 (0.610)	1.60 (1.07)	5.14** (2.30)	2.03 (1.26)

continued

Appendix B Continued

Robustness check 3 OLS regression for democratic quality – 10 years after transition, additional control for WWII (robust standard errors in parentheses)

Independent variables	(1) PY1–3	(2) PY4–6	(3) PY7–10	(4) PY1–10
Prior democratic history				
• Yes	0.127 (0.383)	–0.284 (0.841)	–0.9021 (1.18)	–0.550 (0.735)
per capita GDP	0.000157** (0.000078)	0.000237 (0.000151)	0.00042** (0.00014)	0.000274** (0.00012)
GDP growth rate	1.08 (1.56)	7.90 (4.25)*	3.37 (5.23)	2.33** (0.986)
Constant robust standard error	6.42*** (0.660)	5.12*** (1.08)	3.057 (1.98)	4.69*** (1.12)
R^2	0.32	0.31	0.38	40
N	111	113	112	108

Notes
Significance levels: *** <0.01; ** <0.05; * <0.10 (two-tailed tests).
Model 1 reflects the year 1, 2, 3 Polity average of the dependent variable; Model 2 reflects the year 4, 5, 6 Polity average of the dependent variable.
Model 3 reflects the Year 7, 8, 9, 10 Polity average of the dependent variable; Model 4 reflects the ten-year Polity average of the dependent variable.
Models 1–4 use conversion as the baseline category of the dependent variable. Dataset includes all democratic transitions since 1900.

Robustness check 4 Duration analysis for democratic longevity, with WWII – 10 years after transition

Independent variable	Parameter estimate (hazard ratio)	Robust standard error	Risk ratio (z)	P
Transition Type				
• Conversion	–	–	–	–
• Cooperative	0.053	0.049	–3.18***	0.001
• Collapse	0.408	0.238	–1.53	0.125
• Foreign intervention	0.499	0.337	–1.03	0.304
Institutional choice				
• Parliamentary	5.09	2.56	3.23***	0.001
• Mixed	2.74	1.77	1.56	0.119
Prior Regime Type				
• Single party	1.029	0.535	0.06	0.956
• Personalistic	0.503	0.369	–0.93	0.350
• Colonial history	0.226	0.127	–2.65***	0.008
WWII	0.426	0.254	–1.43	0.153
Prior democratic history				
• Yes	0.690	0.307	–0.83	0.406
per capita GDP	0.999	0.0002	–2.66***	0.008
GDP growth rate	0.284	0.318	–1.12**	0.031

Notes
Number of subjects: 107.
Number of failures: 31.
Time at risk=904.
Wald Chi Squared: 47.14.
Significance levels: *** <0.01; ** <.005; * <0.10.
The model uses conversion as baseline transition category and reflects the GDP per capita average over ten years, in addition to ten-year GDP growth rate.

Index

Page numbers in *italics* denote tables, those in **bold** denote figures.

Arab Spring and democratic prospects 78, 83, 84–108; causal factors 95; causes of transitions 94–6; cross-class coalitions importance 86; economic development factor 94, 108; Egypt *see* Egypt and democratic prospects; institutional approach 95; Libya *see* Libya and democratic prospects; modes of transition 84; Muslim population as possible determent to democracy 94; peaceful versus violent transitions 83; political economy approach 95–6; process-driven approach 95; social groups who bring about regime transitions 96; social media contribution to 101; start of 83; Tunisia *see* Tunisia and democratic prospects; Yemen *see* Yemen and democratic prospects

Austria and Polity score example 57

authoritarian regimes: democratic successors versus 2, 4, 5, 19; transitions and 59

balance of power as important factor in transitions 40

Brazil and political pacts 6

Chile 53

China and democratic prospects 108–13; converted versus cooperation transition 112, 113; creditor nation, as largest 108; dependence on the state 110–11; economic performance and government's credibility 109–10; economics 108, 109; factors favorable to democratic transition 111–12; factors unfavorable to democratic transition 109–11; GDP 108, *109*, 109, 112; as

party-state 110–11, 112; political culture changes 111; political elite and economic development 110; Polity score 112, *113*, 113; populace questioning official ideology 111; social media 111, 112, 20th Party Conference as possible catalyst 112; value model of, predicted 112, *113*; as world factory 108, 109

civil strife, reason for 43

collapse mode of transition 25–6; failure of 121; foreign intervention and violenttransition and 37–9; as independent variable 52; Libya as example of 91; robustness check *130, 131, 133*; survival estimates **65**; unified approach **44**; violent transitions and 33, **33**

competition suppression 42–4

conclusions for book 119–24; democratic transitions 120–1; goal of book 123–4; modes of democratic transition 121, 123; power advantages among incumbents and opposition groups 121; prior regime types and democratic success 122; regime transitions defined 120

consolidation, democratic **16**, 27–8, 29n1; definitions 27–8; military dictatorship effect on 70; pacted transitions and 67

constitutions, drafting new 34, 35

conversion/converted transitions 3–4, 24–6; Chile as example of 53; concern of 122; cooperative transitions versus 67, 68, 70; countries examples 24–5; definition 24; Europe and 72; exclusionary politics and 43; failure rate of pact with 68; as inclusive 41; incumbent led transitions as 41; as independent variable 52; as least

inclusive 36; negotiation and 32; pacts as subset of 24; prior regime type and *71*; regime 24, 33; robustness check *130, 131, 132*; survival estimates **65**; unified approach **44**
cooperative transition 25; beneficial type, as most 46, 121–2; conversion transition versus 67, 68; countries examples 25; definition 25; democratic duration by **8**; democratic quality by **8**; democratic success and 8, 9, 69; duration hypothesis 46, 47, 62, 64; Egypt as example of 102; exclusionary transitions and 43; hypotheses for 46–8; as ideal trajectory of governance 47; as inclusionary 4, 36, 46, 122; as independent variable 52; issues, bargaining over 32–3; as longest lasting survival 48; negotiation and 32, 44–5; opposition forces and 41–2; peaceful 39; Polity scores 65, 67; prior regime type and *71*, 74; quality hypothesis 46, 62, 64, 65, 69; regime-opposition 42; reversion rate 122; robustness check *130, 131, 133*; South Korea as example of 25; success of 123; survival estimates **65**, 69; terms for, other 25; Tunisia as 87; types of transitions statistics summary *7*; unified approach **44**; Yemen as example of 93, 106
Czechoslovakia and Polity score example 57

debate on transitions 4–9
democratic duration by transition type average **8**
democratic growth after transition, prototype **47**
democratic prospects *see* prospects, democratic
democratic quality by transition type average **8**
democratic transition definitions 1, 2, 16, 19
democratic transition modes *see* modes of democratic transition
democratic transitioning states (1900–1999) *125–9*
democratization steps 79

East Germany as example of: short transition period 55; transition from below 20; triggering event for start of transition 21

economic development and democracy 17–18
Egypt and democratic prospects 78, 87–9, 99–102, *102*, 107; coalition, breadth of 87; cooperative transition 102; economic conditions deteriorating 99–100; elections 89; government overthrown 87; military neutrality 88–9, 102; military remained in control problem 89, 102; Muslim Brotherhood and 101–2; Polity score 102, *102*; President Hosni Mubarak resignation 87, 88; protests activities and socioeconomic conditions 87; social media 100–1; Tunisia revolution effect on 99; unemployment 99–100; wealth and corruption disparities 100; youth as face of the movement 87
electoral laws/rules or systems: comments and 41; entering politics or not and 1; founding election 44; importance of in shaping political parties 41, 48n3; importance of negotiation for 40; institutions and 34–5; interim governments and 43; regime conversion and 41
elite led transitions 41–2
embedding democracy in a society 27
ethnically diverse countries and foreign intervention 38
exclusion and inclusionary mechanisms *see* inclusionary and exclusionary mechanisms

focus on transitions 2–4
foreign interventions 26; areas not likely to transition from 72; cooperative transitions and 8, 9; definition 37; ethnically diverse countries and 38; fallout from 37; favorable and unfavorable reasons 38; forcing states by 80; as inclusionary 36; as independent variable 52; Iraq and 78, 79, 80; military regimes and 70; Polity score and 67; prior regime type and *71*; robustness check *130, 131, 132*; single party regimes and 72; statistics 7; survival estimate **65**; unified approach **44**; violent transitions and 33, **33**, 37–9
fortifying democracy 34–5
Freedom House for analyzing country's level of democracy 53–4
frozen democracy 6

goal of book 123–4
Greece from democracy back to
    dictatorship 7, 55
gross domestic product (GDP): China and
    108, *109*, 109; Iraq and 82; Libya and
    104, *104*; Middle East and 81; per capita
    and annual economic growth rates 61;
    Polity score and 68–9; as sustainable
    democracy factor 69, 78

Haiti as example of foreign intervention
    38, 52
Hungary as example of transition from
    above 20

importance of understanding transitions
    9–10
inclusionary and exclusionary
    mechanisms: conversion transition and
    41; cooperative transition and 42;
    exclusionary versus inclusionary 36, 40;
    pacts and 39; as key to success 36–42;
    peaceful transitions by conversion and
    cooperation 39–42; violent transition by
    collapse and foreign intervention 37–9
incumbent-led pacts 24, 39, 40, 68
incumbent-led transitions 42, 46
institutional approach to democracy 95
institutional change 34–5, 44, 67, 68
interim transitional government and
    suppression of competition 43
introduction 1–15; debate on transitions
    4–9; focus on transitions 2–4;
    implementation of democracy 1;
    importance of transitions 9–10; outline
    for 11; regime transition 2, 3
Iranian Revolution triggering event 56
Iraq: democratic prospects 78, 79–83;
    democratic transition predicted value
    model 82–3, *83*; economic potential 82;
    foreign intervention 78, 79, 80; GDP
    growth 82; oil reserves 80–1; oil
    revenues 82; Polity score 56, 74n4, *83*;
    prerequisites for democratic system
    missing 79

knowing where you are going importance
    3

liberation 20
Libya and democratic prospects 78, 89–92,
    102, 103–4, *104*, 106; antigovernment
    protests 89; as collapse transition 91;
    corruption perception index 102; cross-
class coalitions importance 90, 91;
    economic conditions, deteriorating 103;
    GDP 104, *104*; Jasmine Revolution
    inspiration 103; military 90–1; National
    Conference for the Libya Opposition 90;
    NATO 90, 91; Polity score 104, *104*;
    regime overthrown through violence in
    79, 83; revolution start 90; stability
    question 92; tribes importance 90, 103;
    value model of, predicted *104*

Marx on economic change and democracy,
    Karl 17
military and single party: duration
    hypothesis 63; quality hypothesis 63
mixed transitions 53
modernization theories 17, 18, 95
modes of democratic transition 16–31;
    advancing debate 28–9; collapse *see*
    collapse mode of transition;
    consolidation *see* consolidation,
    democratic; conversion *see* conversion/
    converted transitions; cooperative *see*
    cooperative transition; duration analysis
    for democratic longevity of 67; as factor
    in predicting future 39; foreign
    intervention 26; impact of type for
    success or failure 121, 123; importance
    question 61, 62; as intervening variable
    46; outline for 11; preconditions **16**,
    17–9; process *see* process of
    democratization; on shaping of 1; steps
    see steps of democratization, three;
    survival estimates by transition types **65**,
    69; sustainability of democracy and role
    of 123; unified approach **44**
Muslim nation and negative impact on
    democratic transitions 60

national resources impact on growth 81
negotiated agreements/transitions:
    authoritarian regime and 20; balance of
    power as greatest problem in 52;
    bargaining 40; democratic crafting
    involving 19; incumbent-led 24; interim
    governments and 43; peaceful transitions
    and 32, 39; violent transitions and 43

opposition-led negotiated pact 25, 39
ordinary lease squares regression for
    democratic quality table *66*

pacts/pacted transitions 4–6, 7; consolidated
    democracies and 67, 68; cooperative pact

and democracy 70; definition 4; depression of level of inter-party competition by 12n2; exclusionary mechanisms and 39; failure rate of conversion by 68; favorable versus detrimental to democracy 39; frozen democracy and 68; incumbent-led negotiated pacts 24, 39, 40, 68; key to 40; negotiation and 39, 43; opposition-led 39; reduction of mass participation and inclusion by 12n2; as subset of converted and cooperative modes 24; suppression of competition by 5; violence and absence of 39; vital interests and 68

Panama: as example of foreign intervention 52; as example of power struggle after the fall 37–8

parliamentary versus presidential democracies 60, 69

path to transition 4, 19

peaceful and violent transitions 2, 32–3, 121; classifying **33**; conversion and cooperation for peaceful transitions 39–42; democracies versus dictatorship 10; examples 2, 3, 23; features, distinguishing 32; institutional change and 34; negotiation and 32, 39; pacted transitions and 5; results with less violence 36; revolutions 3; single party regimes and peaceful transitions 72; violent versus peaceful transitions 40

peaceful military transition hypothesis 47, 62, 70

peaceful single party regime transition hypothesis 47, 48, 62, 72

Philippines: as example of collapsed transition 26; Polity scores and 74n4

political arrangements 2

political competition: civil conflict and 43; limitations 42; in new democracy 43

political economy approach to democracy 95–6

Polity IV Country Reports 51

Polity IV index for analyzing country's level of democracy 53–4

Polity IV scores: China 112, *113*, 113; conversion transition and 7; definitions 12n5, 48n4; democratic prospects and 78; Egypt 102, *102*; GDP and 68–9; interruption in 74n4; Iraq 83, *83*; Libya 104, *104*; prior democratic history and 59; research design and empirics and 54–8; Tunisia 98–9; Yemen 106, *106*

Portugal and Polity score example 57

posttransitional definition 75n9

preconditions for democratization 17–19

presidential versus parliamentary democracies 60, 69

process of democratization 19–23; areas 16; time continuum **16**

process-driven elite strategic choice 18–19, 95

prospects, democratic 78–118; Arab Spring *see* Arab Spring and democratic prospects; China *see* China and democratic prospects; Iraq *see* Iraq and democratic prospects; outline 12

prototype democratic growth after transition **47**

regime transition: categories of 28–9; collapse of 28–9; definitions 16, 32, 120; duration analysis for democratic longevity table *67*; incumbent-led negotiated pacts sub-category 24; introduction 2; political process and 41; retaining monopoly of power resources 41; single party 72, 78; social groups who bring about 96; types transitioning 44–6, **46**, 47

regime types, prior 44–6, **46**; cooperative transitions and 74; as determining transition type 47, 61, 122; duration analysis results and 72, *74*; logistic regression result on transition type *71*; Polity score 68; results for democratic quality and 72, *73*; robustness check *131*, *133*

research design and empirics 51–77; analysis 65–74; dependent and independent variable coding rules *58*; dependent variable 53–7; empirical results and analysis 61–4; GDP per capita and annual economic growth rates 61; independent variables 52–3, 57, 59–61; institutional choice 60–1; outline 11–2; Polity score and dependent variable 53–8; Polity score and independent variables 57, 58, 59; prior democratic history 59; prior regime type 57; region 59–60; statistical methodology 64–5

revolutions: as least problematic transition type 6; Romania example 3; troublesome issue with 3

robustness checks for: democratic longevity, with World War II *133*; democratic quality *130*;

robustness checks for *continued*
duration analysis for democratic
longevity *130*; regression for democratic
quality *131–2*
Romania as triggering event for transition
example 21–2

smooth monotonic transitions 36
social class manoeuvering 18
social groups who bring about regime
transition 96
social media role in: Arab Spring 101;
China 111, 112; Egyptian government
overthrow 100–1; Libya revolution
102–4; Tunisia revolution 97–8; Yemen
revolution 105
South Korea as example of cooperative
transition 25
start of transition signs 19–20
statistical: analysis goal 63; methodology
64–5
statistics of transitions types summary *7*
steps of democratization, three:
consolidation 27–8; preconditions 17–9;
process of transition 19–23
Sub-Saharan Africa Polity score 68
success rate of democratic transitions,
theory explaining 32–50; classifying **33**;
hypotheses 46, 47–8; inclusionary and
exclusionary mechanisms *see*
inclusionary and exclusionary
mechanisms as key to success;
institutions 34–5; outline for 11; prior
regime type 44, 45–6, **46**; suppressing
competition 42–4; violent and peaceful
transitions 32–3
suppressing competition 42–4
survival estimates by transition type **65**, 69

Taiwan: determining trigger event 55; as
incumbent-elite-led process 55; Polity
score 55; as transition by conversion
example 24–5; as triggering event for
transition example 21, 22, 23
theory explaining success rate of democratic
transitions *see* success rate of democratic
transitions, theory explaining
timing variance from triggering event (s)
to transition examples 21–3
totalitarian regime path to democracy 45–6
transition process definition 19
trigger event for: Chile 53; determining
when process of democracy starts 21–2,
23, 52; Iran 56

Tunisia and democratic prospects 78,
84–7, 96–9, 107; abdication of President
Zine el Abidine Ben Ali 84, 85; Ben
Achour Commission 85; chance for
democracy, optimistic 98; as
cooperative transition 87; cross-class
coalitions 86–7; economic conditions,
deteriorating 96–7; Jasmine Revolution
84; military 85; nonviolent shift 86;
Polity score 98–9; regime change
starting point 84; regional disparity 97;
self-immolation of Mohamed Bouazizi
84, 97; social media role 97–8;
unemployment problem 97; value model
of democratic transition, predicted *99*;
WikiLeaks release of secret cables 97

United States military intervention 80
U.S.S.R. and incumbent-led transition 46

Venezuela oil wealth and democratization
82
violent and peaceful transitions 2, 32–3,
121; classifying **33**; collapse and foreign
intervention, violent transitions by 37–9;
examples 2, 3, 23; democracies versus
dictatorship 10; features, distinguishing
32; inclusionary and exclusionary
mechanisms and 36; institutional change
and 34; interim governments and 43;
Libya violent regime change 83;
military regimes transition through
violence 70, 72; negotiation and 32, 43;
pacted transitions and 5; peaceful versus
violent transitions 40; results with less
violence 36; revolutions 3; uncertainty
with violent transitions 37
violent personalistic transition hypothesis
47, 62, 70

Yemen and democratic prospects 78, 92–4,
104, 105–6, *106*; Arab Spring
inspiration 105; assassination attempt on
President Ali Abdullah Saleh 92, 93; as
cooperative transition 106; corruption
and injustice 105; defections 93;
demonstrations 105; economic
conditions, deteriorating 105; GDP 105,
106, *106*; Gulf Cooperation Council
(GCC) 93; initial protests 92; military
92, 93; Polity score 106, *106*; reasons
for uprising 104, 105; regime overthrow
92; social media 105; value model of,
predicted *106*